MW01169402

前环衬页:不识庐山真面目

Front jacket lap: The True Features of →
Mt. Lushan is Hard to See

联合国教育、科学及文化组织
UNITED NATIONS EDUCATIONAL, SCIENTIFIC
AND CULTURAL ORGANISATION

　　世界遗产公约的标志,它象征着文化遗产与自然遗产之间相互依存的关系。中央的正方形是人类创造的形状,圆圈代表大自然,两者密切相连。这个标志呈圆形,既象征全世界,也象征着要进行保护。

This emblem symbolizes the interdependence of cultural and natural properties: the central square is a form created by man and the circle represents nature, the two being intimately linked. The emblem is round like the world and at the same time it is a symbol of protection.

中国世界遗产被联合国教科文组织世界遗产委员会
批准列入《世界遗产名录》年表

CHRONOLOGY OF RECOGNITION OF WORLD HERITAGES IN CHINA BY WORLD HERITAGE COMMISION OF UNESCO

遗 产 名 称	批准时间	NAME OF HERITAGES	YEAR OF RECOGNITION
长 城(文化遗产)	1987 年 12 月	The Great Wall (Cultural heritage)	December, 1987
北京故宫(文化遗产)	1987 年 12 月	The Palace Museum in Beijing (Cultural heritage)	December, 1987
敦煌莫高窟(文化遗产)	1987 年 12 月	Mogao Grottoes in Dunhuang (Cultural heritage)	December, 1987
秦始皇陵及兵马俑坑(文化遗产)	1987 年 12 月	Qin Shi Huang's Mausoleum and his Terracotta Army (Cultural heritage)	December, 1987
周口店北京人遗址(文化遗产)	1987 年 12 月	Zhoukoudian – Home of Peking man (Cultural heritage)	December, 1987
泰山风景名胜区(文化和自然双重遗产)	1987 年 12 月	Mount Taishan (Both a Cultural and a natural heritage)	December, 1987
黄山风景名胜区(文化和自然双重遗产)	1990 年 12 月	Huangshan Mountain (Both a Cultural and a natural heritage)	December, 1990
武陵源风景名胜区(自然遗产)	1992 年 12 月	Wulingyuan Scenic Area (Natural heritage)	December, 1992
九寨沟风景名胜区(自然遗产)	1992 年 12 月	Jiuzhaigou Scenic Area (Natural heritage)	December, 1992
黄龙风景名胜区(自然遗产)	1992 年 12 月	Yellow Dragon Scenic Area (Natural heritage)	December, 1992
承德避暑山庄及周围寺庙(文化遗产)	1994 年 12 月	Chengde Mountain Resort and Temples Around it (Cultural heritage)	December, 1994
曲阜孔庙、孔府、孔林(文化遗产)	1994 年 12 月	Confucius Temple, Residence and Confucian Woods (Cultural heritage)	December, 1994
武当山古建筑群(文化遗产)	1994 年 12 月	Ancient Architecture in Wudang Mountain (Cultural heritage)	December, 1994
布达拉宫(文化遗产)	1994 年 12 月	Potala Palace of Lhasa (Cultural heritage)	December, 1994
庐山风景名胜区(文化景观遗产)	1996 年 12 月	Mount Lushan (Cultural landscape heritage)	December, 1996
峨眉山—乐山大佛(文化和自然双重遗产)	1996 年 12 月	Mount Emei and the Giant Buddha of Leshan (Both a Cultural and natural heritage)	December, 1996

世界遗产在中国

World Heritage in China

游 琪 主编

Editor-in-Chief You Qi

中 国 旅 游 文 化 学 会

北京五色土旅游文化有限责任公司 合编

Edited by China Tourism Culture Society
Beijing Wusetu Tourism Culture Corporation Ltd

旅游教育出版社

中国·北京

TOURISM EDUCATION PRESS

Beijing, China

摄影者及资料提供者名单
（以姓氏笔画为序）

丁长征	孔祥林	王五龙	王恒来	田 波
李 冬	李建军	李印德	李天社	李延国
刘光辉	刘建军	汪根华	汪传树	闵海生
张文立	张永福	张用衡	张登山	张伟文
陈守清	陈克寅	陈淑华(女)		罗哲文
罗娅玲(女)		罗克恒	郭泽民	郭道明
杨异同	林 萌	胡 锤	赵辉廷	
曹菲(女)	崔贵海	殷锡翔	熊元生	

PHOTOGRAPHERS AND SUPPLIERS OF MATERIAL
(listed according to strokes of surname)

Ding Changzheng   Kong Xianglin

Wang Wulong   Wang Henglai

Tian Bo   Li Dong   Li Jianjun

Li Yinde   Li Tianshe   Li Yanguo

Liu Guanghui   Liu jianjun   Wang Genhua

Wang Chuanshu   Min Haisheng

Zhang Wenli   Zhang Yongfu

Zhang Yongheng   Zhang Dengshan

Zhan Weiwen   Cheng Shouqin

Chen Keyin   Chen Shuhua(f)

Luo Zhewen   Luo Yaling(f)

Luo Keheng   Guo Zemin   Guo Daoming

Yang Yitong   Lin Meng   Hu Chui

Zhao Huiting   Cao Fei(f)   Cui Guihai

Yin Xixiang   Xiong Yuansheng

目　录

CONTENTS

中華奇葩，
世界遺産。

The world heritages in China is erudite and profound.

中华人民共和国文化部部长　刘忠德题词

Inscription by Liu Zhongde
Minister of Culture of the People's Republic of China

愿更多的中华古迹和自然景区
列入《世界遗产目录》，让更多的
世界人民共享中华之明的宝库及
领略中国风光之神采。

韦钰
九七年二月

中国联合国教科文组织全国委员会主任　韦　钰题词

Inscription by Wei Yu

Chairwoman of Chinese National Commission for
UNESCO

中国的世界文化和
自然遗产是珍贵的
旅游资源。

何光暐

一九九七年二月十五日

The cultural properties of China are precious tourist resources.

中华人民共和国国家旅游局局长　　何光暐题词
Inscription by He Guangwei
Director of National Tourism Administration of
the People's Republic of China

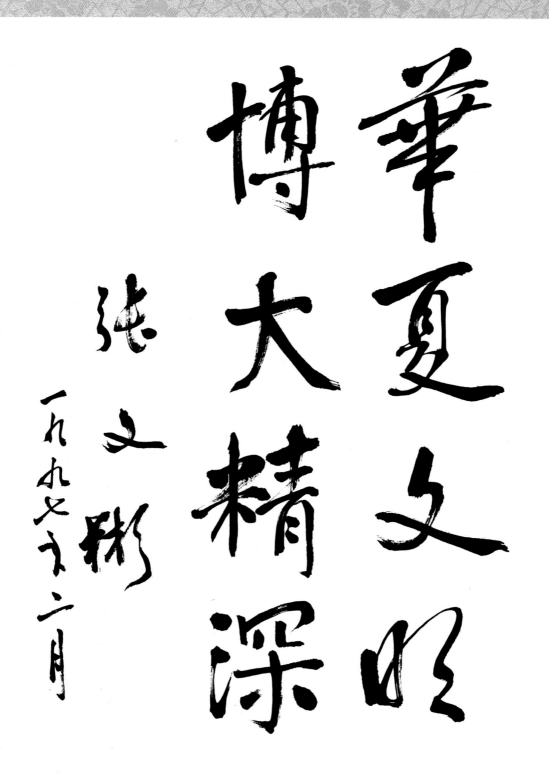

華夏文明
博大精深

張文彬

一九九七年二月

The civilization of ancient China is erudite and profound.

中华人民共和国国家文物局局长　　张文彬题词
Inscription by Zhang Wenbih
Director of State Bureau of Cultural Relics of the
People's Republic of China

写在出版之前

　　也许是天意,正当我们积极操作,准备赶在 1996 年底前发稿时,得知 12 月 5 日在墨西哥召开的联合国教科文组织世界遗产委员会会议将讨论通过一批列入《世界遗产名录》的世界文化和自然遗产,其中有两处是我国的文化景观遗产庐山和文化与自然双重遗产峨眉山—乐山大佛,这是我国自 1986 年以来向联合国教科文组织申报的第七批世界遗产项目,很有可能得到批准。于是我们推迟发稿,搜集这两处的图文资料,等待结果。会议结束,消息传来,不出所料,两处遗产双双被批准列入《世界遗产名录》,从而使我国列入《名录》的文物古迹和自然景观达到 16 处,也使我们这本《世界遗产在中国》成为我国第一本收编最全的图册。

　　保护世界文化与自然遗产,是联合国教科文组织多年来积极开展的一项意义重大、影响深远的国际合作活动。1972 年 11 月,联合国教科文组织第 17 届大会通过了《保护世界文化和自然遗产公约》(简称《世界遗产公约》)。这项公约得到了国际社会的普遍承认和支持。迄今为止,世界上共有 147 个国家批准或加入公约,成为公约的缔约国。为有效地实施《世界遗产公约》,联合国教科文组织于 1976 年成立了一个政府间合作机构——世界遗产委员会,由公约缔约国大会选举产生的 21 个国家组成,其主要任务之一是在缔约国提出建议的基础上,确定应在《世界遗产公约》范围内加以保护的各国文化和自然遗产,将这些国际公认的具有突出意义和普遍价值的文物古迹和自然景观列入《世界遗产名录》,使国际社会将其作为人类的共同遗产加以保护。截至 1996 年底,全世界共有 506 处文化和自然遗产被联合国教科文组织世界遗产委员会批准列入《世界遗产名录》,其中文化遗产 380 处,自然遗产 107 处,文化与自然双重遗产 19 处,分布在世界五大洲约 110 个国家。

　　我国有五千年古老灿烂的文化,拥有十分丰厚的文化遗产和壮丽多姿的自然风光。我国政府一向重视文化和自然遗产的保护工作,积极支持和参与联合国教科文组织保护世界文化和自然遗产的国际合作活动。1985 年 11 月,全国人民代表大会常务委员会批准了联合国教科文组织的《世界遗产公约》,我国成为公约的缔约国之一。1986年以来,我国政府先后分七批向联合国教科文组织申报世界遗产项目。截至1996年12月,我国加入《世界遗产公约》的11年中,就有16处文物古迹和自然景观列入《世界遗产名录》,这一成就令世人瞩目,中国作为世界遗产大国的地位受到国际社会的普遍重视。中华光辉灿烂的文化属于中华全民族,也是全人类的珍贵遗产。相信我国会有更多的古迹和景观相继被批准列入《世界遗产名录》。

本图册按遗产被批准的先后次序排列,以图文并茂、中英文对照的形式出版,以便为国内外更多的人了解我国珍贵的世界遗产提供方便。

我们感谢几位主管部、局的领导人为本图册题词,感谢中国联合国教科文组织全国委员会马燕生,建设部曹南燕,国家文物局郭旃、詹德华帮助审稿和在本图册编辑过程中所给予的协助。特别感谢文物专家罗哲文先生帮助审稿并提供资料和珍藏的照片,使我们有可能把从公元前7世纪至4世纪春秋战国时期起始修建,历经两千多年营造,横跨16个省、市、自治区各个时期所建的长城,累计长度超过5万多公里的全貌介绍给读者。帮助审稿的还有文物专家黄景略先生。图册的英文翻译由外文局中国文学杂志社译审、中国作协彩虹翻译终身成就奖获得者喻璠琴担任,在此一并致谢。也感谢所有为本图册的出版付出过爱心的人。

谨以此图册献给一切为保护世界遗产作出贡献的人们!

游 琪

1997,2

A NOTE BEFORE PUBLICATION

At a time when we all pitched in to have the manuscripts ready before the year 1996 drew to a close, we had the good luck to learn that on December 5 the World Heritage Commission for the United Nations Educational, Scientific and Cultural Organization (UNESCO) was meeting in Mexico to discuss the inclusion of a new batch of cultural and natural properties in the *List of World Heritages*. Since 1986 China has submitted heritages for consideration seven times. Among the list this time were Mount Lushan — a cultural landscape heritage and Mount Emei — Giant Buddha of Leshan — both a cultural and a natural heritage. And they had a good chance too. Accordingly, we set out to collect pictures and materials about these sites and waited patiently for the outcome. News finally came that both were accepted, thus making China a country with 16 cultural and natural properties included in the *List of World Heritages*. It also made this book the first one in China complete with all world heritages in China.

For many years, UNESCO has promoted a highly significant international activity concerning the preservation of the world's cultural and natural properties. In November 1972, the 17th UNESCO Conference adopted the "Preservation of the World Cultural and Natural Heritage Treaty" (the "World Heritage Treaty" in short) which won international recognition and support. Up till now, 147 countries have been accepted as signatories to the Treaty. To ensure the effective implementation of the Treaty, UNESCO set up in 1976 the World Heritage Commission — an intergovernmental organization made up of 21 countries chosen by a conference of the signatories. One of its main task is to determine, on the basis of the signatories' submission what should be under the Treaty's protection and then include in the *List of World Heritages* those cultural relics and natural sceneries which are internationally recognized as having outstanding significance and of common value. The aim is to place these common heritages of mankind under protection. By the end of 1996, the commission has adopted 506 world heritages from 110 countries in five continents. Among them 380 are cultural properties, 107 are natural properties, 19 are both cultural and natural properties.

China has a culture dating back 5,000 years, she is a country with a wealth of cultural properties and natural sceneries. The Chinese government has allways laid stress on the preservation of these properties and has actively supported and participated in international activities organized by UNESCO in this field. In November 1985, the Standing Committee of the National People's Congress of China approved UNESCO's World Heritage Treaty, making China one of its signatories. Since 1986, China has submitted seven batches of world heritages for UNESCO's consideration. It is quite amazing that by December 1996, a more 11 years after China's participation in the Treaty, 16 of her cultural relics and natural sceneries were included in the *List of World Heritages*. As a country with a large number of would heritages, China is attracting international attention. China's brilliant ancient culture belongs to the entire Chinese nation. It is also a precious heritage of the whole mankind. We are confident that many more cultural and natural properties of China will be included in the *List of World Heritages* by UNESCO.

Arranged in the order of the inclusion of these heritages this book aims to facilitate the learning of our precious heritages by more people at home and abroad through a wide range of pictures and Chinese and English texts.

We wish to thank leaders in concerned ministries and bureaus for their inscriptions for this book. We also wish to express our gratitude to Ma Yansheng of Chinese National Commission for UNESCO, Cao Nanyan of the Ministry of Construction and Guo Zhan and Zhan Dehua of the State Bureau of Cultural Relics who helped us with the editorial work. We particularly appreciate Luo Zhewen, an expert in cultural relics, who not only went through our manuscripts but also supplied us with precious material and pictures in his collection, thus making it possible for us to introduce to our readers the Great Wall, the construction of which lasted two thousand years from the 7th century BC to the 4th century, a Great Wall spanning 16 provinces, municipalities and autonomous regions and adding up to a total length of over fifty thousand kilometers. We also wish to thank Huang Jinglue, a specialist in cultural relics, who went through our manuscripts too. Our thanks also go to Yu Fanqin, senior translator of Chinese Literature Press and winner of the Rainbow Prize for her lifelong achievements in translation sponsored by the Chinese Writers Association, for translating this book into English. We appreciate all who have shown concern for the publication of this book in various stages.

We wish to dedicate this book to all who have made contributions to the conservation of world heritages.

YOU QI

February, 1997

八达岭长城
Badaling Great Wall

长　　城
THE GREAT WALL

　　横亘于中国崇山峻岭、河流峡谷、沙漠高原之间的长城在中国境内绵延数万里。其内涵丰富、历史久远、姿态万千、景色壮观。是世界上伟大的古代军事防御体系。

　　长城大约开始修筑于中国公元前 7 至 4 世纪的春秋战国时期，为防御外来侵掠，许多诸候国开始在边境营造数百里或上千里的不封闭的城墙，这种城墙就是中国最早修建的长城。最早修筑长城的是楚国。公元前 221 年秦始皇统一中国后，将原有的北方的秦、赵、燕三国长城连接起来并加固、增建，西起临洮（今甘肃岷县），向东达辽东，长万余里，形成当时的"万里长城"。汉朝为防御北方游牧民族南下对农耕地区的掠扰，建筑了防边长城的障、城、亭、燧等军事防御设施。汉长城东起辽东，西经盐泽（今新疆罗布泊），向西继之以烽燧，直到新疆的西部，全长超过二万里。作为中国古代重要的防卫工事，长城经北魏、北齐、东魏、北周、

隋朝、辽朝、金朝、明朝等各个历史阶段，长达二千多年间的营造。特别是明代二百多年间浩大的长城修筑工程，东起鸭绿江，西到嘉峪关，全长 6300 多公里，被称为"万里长城"，并设立了辽东镇、蓟镇、宜府镇、大同镇、山西镇、延绥镇、宁夏镇、固原镇、甘肃镇等九个防守区，亦称"九边"、"九镇"，有效地对长城全线进行防务管理和修筑，形成了由城墙、关、城堡、墙台和烟墩等组成的完整防御工程体系。我们今天看到的长城多是这一时期修筑的。经实地考察已证实，横跨中国黑龙江、吉林、辽宁、河北、北京、天津、山西、内蒙古、河南、陕西、山东、湖北、湖南、宁夏、甘肃、新疆等省、市、自治区各个时期的长城累计长度达五万多公里以上。

　　历代递建的长城始终遵循就地取材、因地制宜的原则，建筑材料与形式多以土、石为主，但也因自然条件的差别而异。城墙是长城的主体，最早是利用生土夯筑，后则加工为石，同时又根据个别地段的地质特点，或以木板、木榨等构筑墙体，或利用山岭的自然形态为墙体，建筑材料不限于土、石，丰富多变的特点在

今天仍可清晰看到。秦汉长城多以自然石块垒砌，或夯土修筑尽量利用山险建成，在山脊、悬崖峭壁处，多利用地形，稍加修缀而成墙体。而在风蚀严重的草原、荒漠地区，常用土坯筑成甚至还有用苇草层或红柳层的夹筑砂砾墙体，如今甘肃省玉门关一带的长城。金代长城主要分布在少石多土的内蒙古高原上，多以夯土版筑或土坯做墙。明长城在山区一般利用山脊作墙基，外包砌条石、青砖，内填黄土、碎石，既便于施工，又节省材料和劳力，如居庸关八达岭长城；或用砖砌成墙体两侧，内填黄土、碎石，如河北省山海关到山西省雁门关一带的长城。长城沿线还因地理位置的重要程度建有规模不等的其他各类防御设施，如关、城堡、墙台和烽火台等，在军事上满足驻兵、屯粮、防卫、藏武器和军情传递的需要。

历史上的长城作为农耕民族与游牧民族两大经济区域文化冲撞与融合的产物，为推动中原地区经济发展及文明进程，稳固统一多民族国家的形成与发展，保障中西交通要道"丝绸之路"的畅通起到了重要的推动作用。今天的长城虽已失去了昔日的功能，但已作为中华民族古老文化的丰碑、各族人民共同劳动的结晶，与埃及的金字塔，罗马的斗兽场、比萨斜塔等被誉为世界奇迹，象征着中华民族血脉相承的聪明智慧和民族精神。

Rising and falling along lofty ridges and towering ranges, twisting and turning across deserts and plateaus for thousands of kilometers, the Great Wall of China is a fantastic sight. It has a rich connotation, agelong history, magnificent surrounding scenes and a thousand different poses and appearances. It is a great military defensive system of the world built in ancient times.

Around the 7th to the 4th century BC during the Spring and Autumn Period, to ward off plundering nomadic people living in the north, ducal states began to build walls at their borders running several hundred kilometers long. The State of Chu was the first to build such walls. In 221 BC, when Qin Shi Huang conquered all the other six ducal states and became the first emperor of a unified China, he had the walls of the three northern states of Qin, Zhao and Yan linked up, reinforced and extended. It finally ran over ten thousand *li* (one *li* equals to 0.5 kilometer) from Lintao (present-day Minxian, Gansu Province) in the west to Liaodong in the east.

During the Han Dynasty (206 BC - 220 AD) which followed the Qin (221 BC-206 BC), in order to protect the farming areas from the harassment of nomadic people, the Han emperors constructed military defensive works like castles, battlements, fortifications and beacon towers along the wall which started in Liaodong in the east and ran on to Yanze (present-day Lop Nur in Xinjiang), Fengsui, until the western part of Xinjiang with a total length over 10,000 kilometers. The construction of the Great Wall went on for over two thousand years through various historical periods including Northern Wei, Northern Qi, Eastern Wei, Northern Zhou, Sui, Liao, Kin and particularly during the Ming Dynasty whose rule lasted over two hundred years. It was then over 6,300 kilometers from Yalu River in the east to Jiayuguan in the west and became known as the Great Wall of Ten Thousand *Li*. Nine garrison areas were set up to carry out effective control and repairs of the entire wall. They were Liaodong, Jizhou, Xuanfu, Datong, Shanxi, Yansui, Ningxia, Guyuan and Gansu, forming a complete defensive system with walls, passes, castles, strategic platforms and beacon towers. Most parts of the Great Wall we see today were constructed in this period. Investigations show that the walls spanning

Heilongjiang, Jilin, Liaoning, Hebei, Beijing, Tianjin, Shanxi, Inner Mongolia, Henan, Shaanxi, Shandong, Hubei, Hunan, Ningxia, Gansu, Xinjiang, etc. during various periods add up to over 50,000 kilometers.

Through the dynasties, the construction of the Great Wall followed the principal of using local materials where possible. Earth and stones were the most common, other materials were also possible according to natural conditions. The wall, the main body of the Great Wall, was rammed earth in the early period; later stones, in certain sections, planks and boards according to geological characteristics. Natural terrain was also taken advantage of to make up part of the wall. Even today materials other than earth and stone are still discernable. The walls of the Qin and Han dynasties were of rammed earth or rocks while taking advantage of steep mountain ridges and precipices where possible. In grasslands and deserts subjected to wind erosion, the walls were built with unburnt bricks or layers of reeds and tamarisk twigs filled with sand and crushed stones like the Great Wall at Yumenguan in Gansu Province. The Kin Dynasty wall in the Inner Mongolian plateau where stone was scarce was rammed earth and unburnt bricks. In the Ming Dynasty a wall of large slabs of granite and bricks filled in with crushed stones and earth was erected over the contours of mountain ridges like the section between Juyongguan and Badaling which saved material and labour power and was easy to build. The stretch from Shanhaiguan in Hebei to Yanmenguan in Shanxi was bricks filled in with earth and crushed stone. Defensive works like passes, castles, strategic platforms and beacon towers were built along the Great Wall according to the geological importance of the section and to serve the military needs of garrison, grain and weapon storage, defence, and the transmission of military information.

The Great Wall in history, a product of cultural clashes between the agricultural and nomadic peoples, played an important role in propelling the Central Plain's economic development and cultural progress, stabilizing and unifying a multi-national country, and guaranteeing the passage of the "Silk Road" which linked ancient China with the West. The Great Wall today may have lost its former functions, it has nevertheless become a monument of the ancient civilization of the Chinese nation. It is the fruit of concerted labour of various nationalities. Like the pyramids of Egypt, the arena in Roman antiquity and the leaning tower of Pisa, it is one of the wonders of the world, symbolizing the wit and spirit of the Chinese nation.

齐 长 城
THE QI GREAT WALL

　　齐长城为春秋战国时期齐国在约公元前 6 世纪至 5 世纪开始修筑的长城。自山东省平阴县东北至胶南县海滨。最初的长城是利用济水的堤防再筑墙体连结山脉而成。有夯筑和石砌两种，墙厚约 4—5 米。现存残高自 1—2 米至 3—4 米不等，在山东省莱芜、临清等地可见。

　　During the Spring and Autumn and the Warring States period (722BC-221 BC) the State of Qi started building the Great Wall at around the 6th to the 5th century BC. The wall, built on the Jishui River dyke to link up with mountain ranges, stretched from the northeast of Pingying County to the coast of Jiaonan County in Shandong Province. It was built of rammed earth or stone and was 4-5 meters wide. The remains range from one or two meters to three or four meters high. They still exist in Laiwu and Linqing in Shandong Province.

山东黄南齐长城东头（土筑）
↑ Qi Great Wall's eastern section, built of earth, in Huangnan, Shandong Province

山东泰安齐长城中段（石筑）
↖ Qi Great Wall's middle section, built of rock, in Taian, Shandong Province

山东长清齐长城西头（土筑）
← Qi Great Wall's western end, built of earth, in Changqing, Shandong Province

固阳秦长城遗址
REMAINS OF THE QIN GREAT WALL AT GUYANG

位于内蒙古自治区固阳县。现存遗址长约 120 公里,基本延续,高出地面 1 米至数米不等。由石块垒筑,每隔一段建有烽火台,台多在城南侧 50 米之内,台附近设有哨所、哨位。固阳秦长城是研究中国早期长城建筑的重要实物例证。

Located in the Guyang County, Inner Mongolia Autonomous Region, the remains stretch continuously for about 120 kilometers with a height ranging from one to several meters. Beacon Towers with sentinal posts near them are erected at intervals on the stone wall within 50 meters to the south of the county town. This section of the Great Wall is an important object example for studying the construction of the Great Wall in the early days.

内蒙古固阳秦长城
Qin Great Wall in Guyang, Inner Mongolia ↗

内蒙古固阳秦长城断面
A section of Qin Great Wall in Guyang, Inner Mongolia →

内蒙古固阳秦长城
Qin Great Wall in → Guyang, Inner Mongolia

阳关、玉门关及长城烽燧遗址
REMAINS OF BEACON TOWERS AT YANGGUAN AND YUMENGUAN

据历史记载,阳关、玉门关是中国古代通往西域的"丝绸之路"的南、北两个起点,汉长城著名的重要关口。

玉门关位于甘肃省敦煌市西北。相传新疆和田一带出产美玉,路经这里运往中原,故得名玉门关。古往今来人们喜爱的许多诗句更使玉门关名声远扬。玉门关自汉武帝元封三年(公元前108年)设置,从张骞出使西域,开辟"丝绸之路"后,开始繁盛;魏晋南北朝以来,战争频繁,渐衰而废弃。现存小方盘城,东西长24.5米,南北宽26.4米,残高约9米。玉门关附近的长城由红柳条、芦苇和沙砾石叠压筑成,沿线每隔一定距离,便筑有(烽燧)烽火台,当年用于燃点烟火报警通报敌情的积薪芦苇犹清晰可见。

阳关因位于玉门关以南而得名阳关。现存房基和烽燧遗址。

According to historical records, Yangguan and Yumenguan were the two terminals of the Silk Road, one in the south, the other in the north, both strategic passes of the Han Great Wall.

Yumenguan is situated northwest of Dunhuang, Gansu Province. Legend has it that the beautiful jade produced in Hetian, Xinjiang passed through here on its way to the Central Plain. Hence the name Yumen (gate of jade). Its fame spread far and wide for being referred to in many popular poems since ancient times. Established in 108 BC (the third year of the Yuan Feng reign of Emperor Wu Di of Han), it prospered after Zhang Qian, the first envoy of Emperor Wu Di to the western regions, passed here on his journey and opened up the Silk Road. Yet the frequent wars during the Wei, Jin and the Southern and Northern dynasties (220-589) caused its decline. It was finally abandoned.

The Square Fortification we see today is 24.5 meters from west to east and 26.4 meters from north to south. The height of the remains is 9 meters. The Great Wall near Yumenguan was built of sand, crushed stones, tamarisk twigs and reeds. All along the wall, beacon towers were built at intervals. Remains of firewood and reeds used for sending out signals at that time still lie around the place.

Yangguan is situated to the south of Yumenguan. Hence the name Yangguan (the sun). Remains of Yangguan include house foundations and beacon towers.

敦煌西汉玉门关小方盘城
Western Han's Square Fortification →
at Yumenguan, Dunhuang

敦煌西汉阳关遗址
Remains of Western Han Yangguan in Dunhuang ↓

小方盘城内景
Inside View of the Square Fortification ↑

敦煌玉门关芦秆砂砾长城结构
The Great Wall built of reeds and gravel at Yumenguan, Dunhuang ↑

敦煌玉门关积薪
Firewood remains at Yumenguan ↑

丹东虎山明长城遗址
REMAINS OF THE MING GREAT WALL AT TIGER MOUNTAIN IN DANDONG

位于辽宁省丹东市宽甸县虎山。属明长城东段,现地面保存有墙台遗址。

The footing of the eastern section of the Ming Great Wall still exist on Tiger Mountain (Hushan) in Kuandian County, Dandong, Liaoning Province.

明长城东端起点虎山长城遗址
Remains of Hushan Great Wall — the eastern end of Ming Great Wall ↑

明长城东端起点虎山长城遗址
Remains of Hushan Great Wall — the eastern end of Ming Great Wall ↓

明长城东端起点虎山长城遗址
Remains of Hushan Great Wall　the eastern end of Ming Great Wall　↑

明长城起点虎山长城遗址
Remains of Hushan Great Wall — the starting point of Ming Great Wall　↓

山 海 关 长 城
SHANHAIGUAN

　　山海关自古有天下第一关的美誉。位于河北省秦皇岛市东部,系万里长城东端最要冲的关口。明洪武十四年(公元1381年)大将军徐达在此建关设卫,定名山海关。关城呈不规则梯形,设四门,分别称为镇乐、迎恩、望洋、威远。东西门筑有罗城,南北筑有翼城。城墙平均高11.6米,厚10余米,内为土筑,外用砖包。"天下第一关"巨匾系明代书法家萧显所书,置于东门二楼房檐之下。南北有造型相同的牧营、临闾楼,东北、东南转角处建有角楼,彼此呼应,气势恢宏。

　　山海关向东5公里为长城海中起点。砌石为垒,高约10米,入海21米如龙头入海,搅波掀浪故称老龙头。建筑主要包括入海石城、靖卤台、南海关口、澄海楼、宁海城等。

Shanhaiguan became known as the First Pass Under Heaven since ancient times. It is situated in the east of Qinhuangdao City, Hebei Province, forming a pass of strategic importance at the eastern end of the Great Wall. It was set up by General Xu Da in 1381 (the 14th year of the Ming Hong Wu reign) when a castle was erected here.

Shanhaiguan was shaped like an irregular trapezoid with a gate on each side, namely Zhendong, Yingen, Wangyang and Weiyuan. The south and north wings are fortifications where soldiers were stationed. Outside the east and west gates are outer walls to strengthen the defence of the castle. The average height of the Shanhaiguan Great Wall is 11.6 meters, its width over 10 meters. It is built of rammed earth faced with bricks. A horizontal board with the inscription for "First Pass Under Heaven" in the calligraphy of the Ming dynasty scholar Xiao Xian hangs on the second story of the gatetower. There are two small fortifications, one in the south, the other in the north. They are the same shape and size. Together with towers at the northeast and southeast corner, they present a solemn majesty.

Five kilometers to the east of Shanhaiguan, the starting point of the Great Wall dips into the sea like a dragon's head. Piling 10 meters high and dipping 21 meters into the sea, the rocks chum the surging waves. Hence the name Old Dragon Head. It is a complex of a stone fortification, the Jinglu platform, the South sea pass, and the Chenghailou Tower and the Ninghai Castle.

角山长城
Jiaoshan Great Wall　↓

老龙头
Old Dragon Head ↑

天下第一关　　　→
First Pass Under Heaven

29

黄 崖 关 长 城
HUANGYAGUAN

　　黄崖关长城位于天津市蓟县境内。始建于明永乐年间（1403—1424）。此段长城东以悬崖为依，西借峭壁为据。黄褐色的岩石，在夕阳照射下，层层的山体泛着金光，有晚霞照黄崖之称，而得名黄崖关。敌楼掩体、水关烟墩、要塞营盘等各项防御设施完备。全段长城逶迤于崇山峻岭之间，景色独特，尤以凤凰楼、北极阁、长城碑林等景观为最。但由于自然和人为因素受毁坏较严重。在1984年开始的"爱我中华，修我长城活动"中修复了关城和水路关隘，基本恢复了明代黄崖关原貌，并修复了黄崖关长城部分城墙。

　　Located in Jixian County, Tianjin, Huangyaguan began

building during the Ming Yong Le reign. This section of the Great Wall begins with rocky precipices in the east and ends with sheer cliffs in the west. The brown rocks and the mountains reflecting the golden sunrays at dusk gives the pass its name which means brown rocks in Chinese. The pass is complete with watchtowers, barricades, moats, beacon towers and barracks. Meandering along towering mountains, Huangyaguan has a unique scenery represented by Phoenix Pavilion, North Pole Tower and the cluster of steles in particular. Severely demolished by Nature and Man, the castle and the water pass were reconstructed during the activity of "Love China and repair the Great Wall" which started in 1984. They now have a similar appearance to what they had been in the Ming Dynasty.

黄崖关长城
Huangyaguan Great Wall　↓

黄崖关太平寨长城雪景
Huangyaguan Great Wall at Taiping Village After Snow ↑

蓟北雄关牌坊
An archway at Jibei ↓

31

司马台长城
SIMATAI

　　司马台长城位于北京密云县古北口镇与河北滦平县交界处。始建于明洪武初年,全长19公里。整段长城建筑构思精巧,设计奇特。有敌楼35座,座座结构新颖、形态各异。其中望京楼海拔986米,耸峙奇险,登临其上东观"雾灵积雪",西望"卧虎蟠龙",南瞰"水库明珠",北眺"燕山叠翠"。司马台长城景区自然景观独特,天梯、天桥、天池、鸳鸯泉等自然景观与长城人文景观交相辉映。

Located on the boundary of Gubeikou Town, Miyun County, Beijing, and Luanping County, Hebei Province, the 19 kilometer Simatai began in the first year of the Ming Hong Wu reign. The design and construction of this section of the Great Wall are exquisite and striking. Every one of the 35 watchtowers is original and different. The Tower for Viewing the Capital, 986 meters above sea level, is constructed on sheer precipices, commanding a panoramic view of "snow-capped Wuling" in the east, rolling mountains like "crouching tigers and coiling dragons" in the west, a "mirror-like reservoir" in the south and "verdurous Yanshan Mountain" in the north. Just as outstanding are the natural sceneries at Heavenly Ladder, Fairy Bridge, Heavenly Pool and the Spring of Manderin Duck and Drake which compliment the scenes of the man-made Great Wall.

曙 光
Morning glow

险峻的司马台古长城
Precipitous Simatai Great Wall ↑

岁 月
Glorious Years →

33

郁郁葱葱的司马台长城　Simatai with green and luxuriant trees

金山岭长城
JINSHANLING

金山岭长城位于北京市密云县与河北省滦平县交界地带。为古代兵家必争之地。远在北齐、五代、辽、金时便曾设置关隘和修筑长城。明永乐八年（公元1410年）开始在前代长城基础上修筑金山岭长城。因工程较简单，不易防守，明隆庆二年（公元1568年）大将戚继光在蓟州总兵任内又主持修筑。后又由其弟戚继美监修，连续营造达十余年。

在25公里的金山岭长城段，集中了150多座敌楼和墩台，从建筑外观看计有方形楼、圆形楼、扁形楼、拐角楼；从建筑穹顶看计有平顶式、船篷式、穹隆顶式、四角钻天式、八角藻井式等等。体现了多样的风格，为中国长城很具特色的部分。

The Jinshanling Great Wall is located on the boundary between Miyun County, Beijing and Luanping County, Hebei Province. Being a strategic point since ancient times, a pass and wall were built as early as the Northern Qi (550-577), the Five Dynasties (907-979), Liao (907-1125) and Kin (1115-1234) dynasties. In 1410 (the 8th year of the Ming Yong Le reign) Jinshanling was built on the foundation of that old wall. Still too simple to be an effective defensive works, General Qi Jiguang, who was in command of the Jizhou garrison area, took charge to rebuild it in 1568 (the second year of the Ming Long Qing reign). With his brother Qi Jimei succeeding him, construction went on for over a decade.

The Jinshanling Great Wall, 25 kilometers long, has over 150 watchtowers and battlemented platforms. They are designed in a great variety of shapes — square, circular, oval and multi-cornered. Their ceilings are also varied — flat, vaulted, domed, quadrangular or with an octagonal caisson. This is a very characteristic section of the Great Wall which displays a rich variety of architectural style.

金山岭长城大观
A panorama view of Jinshanling Great Wall

金山岭长城之敌楼
Watchtowers of Jinshanling Great Wall　↑

金山岭长城障墙
Barrier Walls at Jinshanling
Great Wall　→

慕 田 峪 长 城
MUTIANYU

慕田峪长城位于成功举办第四次世界妇女大会NGO论坛的北京怀柔县，北齐时期曾在这里修筑过长城，明洪武年间（公元1368年—1398年）大将徐达在北齐长城遗址上修建长城，明永乐二年（公元1404年）建成"慕田峪关"。隆庆二年（公元1568年）大将戚继光由浙闽调任蓟州总兵后继续整修。

此处长城的构筑及军事设施有着独特的风格和特点，因山峦重叠而敌楼密布，墙体多为条石砌筑，垛口为青砖垒砌。长城两侧均有垛口，外侧设有挡马坑，易守难攻。慕田峪长城西接居庸关，东连古北口，被称为拱卫京师、皇陵的北方屏障。

慕田峪长城风景区植被覆盖率达90％以上，松柏苍翠，四季景色绚丽。

Mutianyu is located in Huairou County, Beijing which successfully hosted the NGO Tribune of the United Nation's Fourth World Conference on Women in 1995. Northern Qi (550-577) started to construct a wall here. During the Ming Hong Wu reign (1368-1398), General Xu Da built the Great Wall on its foundation. The Mutianyu Pass was erected in 1404 (the 2nd year of the Ming Yong Le reign). Construction continued when General Qi Jiguang was transferrel to Jizhou to command the garrison area in 1568 (the 2nd year of the Long Qing reign).

The fortifications and the Great Wall here are characterized by many watchtowers on overlapping mountain ranges. The wall, built with slabs of stone, is crenellated on both sides with bricks. Horsetrapping snares outside the wall offer better protection and ward off attacks. With Juyongguan in the west and Gubeikou in the east.

Mutianyu serves as the northern barrier defending the capital and the imperial tombs. With vegetation, green pines and cypresses covering 90 per cent of the area, the sceneries here are beautiful all the year round.

慕田峪长城
Mutianyu Great Wall

慕田峪长城秋色
Mutianyu in Autumn ↑

慕田峪长城之冬 ↓
Mutianyu in Winter

居 庸 关
JUYONGGUAN

居庸关位于北京市昌平县西北部。居庸之称最早见于战国时期的《吕氏春秋》，得名于秦始皇时期，汉代称"居庸关"，三国时称"西关"，北齐时称"纳税关"，唐时称"居庸关"、"蓟门关"或"军都关"，自辽、金、元、明、清至今，均称"居庸关"。

居庸关是长城重要关隘。居庸关关城建于明洪武初年（1368 年），为朱元璋派开国元勋徐达修筑，此后历代有所修建。

现存一过街塔基座，又称云台，建于元至正五年（1345 年），基座上明代以前曾建有喇嘛塔三座，后毁。云台用大理石砌筑，正中辟券门。券门为八边形，门洞内外刻有元代精美佛教图像的石刻。其中四大天王浮雕、六体文字（梵文、藏文、八思巴蒙文、维吾尔文、汉文、西夏文）石刻最为著名。

历史上居庸关周围景色秀美。金代时就以"居庸叠翠"被列为燕京八大景之一。居庸关附近还有许多名胜古迹，如望京石、杨六郎拴马柱、五郎像、穆桂英点将台等，号称七十二景。

Juyongguan lies to the northwest of Changping County, Beijing. The term *juyong,* appearing first in *The Spring and Autumn Annals of Mr Lu* of the Warring States Period, was attached to this pass during Qin Shi Huang's time. In the Han Dynasty it was called Juyongguan, in the Three Kingdom's period the West Pass, in Northern Qi, the Tax Pass, in the Tang Dynasty Juyongguan Pass, Jimen Pass or Jundu Pass. All through Liao, Kin, Yuan, Ming and Qing dynasties to the present day it has been called Juyongguan.

The castle of this important pass of the Great Wall was built in 1368 (the beginning of the Ming Hong Wu reign) by Xu Da, one

居庸关云台
Cloud Terrace at Juyongguan ↓

新修复的居庸关关城城墙
Newly repaired walls of Juyongguan →

of the military commanders who assisted Emperor Hong Wu (named Zhu Yuanzhang) to found the Ming Dynasty. It has been renovated many times afterwards.

What remains today is the Cloud Terrace constructed in 1345 (the 5th year of the Yuan Zhi Zheng reign). It was originally an overpass erected across a street but later only a platform. Before the Ming Dynasty three lamaist pagodas had stood on the platform. They were later destroyed. The Cloud Terrace has a deep gate in the middle. The gate has an arch with eight angles. The gateway is covered with carvings of Yuan Dynasty Buddhist pictures and scriptures. The most outstanding are the four heavenly kings in bas-relief and the Buddhist scriptures in Sanskrit, Tibetan, Mongolian, Uygur, Han and Xixia languages.

Surrounded with beautiful sceneries and "clusters of verdant trees" Juyongguan was considered one of the eight famous scenic spots in Beijing, then called Yanjing, as early as the Kin Dynasty, 800 years ago. The pass is surrounded by 72 sights such as the Rock for Watching Beijing, the post where Yang Liulang hitched his horse, a statue of Wulang, the terrace where Mu Guiying selected generals, etc.

居庸关云台元代石刻天王像
Yuan Dynasty stone carvings of Heavenly Kings on
Juyongguan's Cloud Terrace ↑

居庸关城门瓮城(东门)
Outer fortification of Juyongguan (the east gate) ↑

41

八达岭长城
BADALING

八达岭长城位于北京市延庆县,始建于明代。从明代洪武年间到万历年间(公元 1368 年—1620 年)前后修筑达 18 次之多。八达岭南通北京,北往延庆,西连宣化、大同。因其四通八达,故称八达岭。八达岭长城墙体由巨大整齐的条石筑成外壁,平均高 7.8 米,宽 5.8 米至 6.5 米,城上设有砖砌女墙和垛口,每隔 250 米至 500 米设有敌楼、墙台。岭口城关建于明弘治十八年(公元 1505 年)。八达岭长城是中国长城保存完整,建筑宏伟,景色壮观,地位非常重要的部分。

Construction of Badaling in Yanqing County, Beijing, started in the Ming Dynasty (1368-1644) and underwent 18 rebuilts from the Hong Wu to the Wan Li reign (1368-1620). Badaling leads to Beijing in the south, Yanqing in the north, Xuanhua and Datong in the west. Hence the name Bada means reaching out in all directions. The wall, built with huge stone slabs on the outside, is 7.8 meters high on the average and 5.8-6.5 meters wide. The crenellated wall has parapets; and watchtowers and fighting platforms are built at 250-500 meters intervals. The castle was built in 1505 (the 18th year of the Ming Hong Zhi reign). The best preserved section of the Great Wall, Badaling locates at a very important position and has a beautiful surrounding scenery and its structures show a special grandeur.

八达岭长城夜景
Night Scene of Badaling →

夏日的八达岭长城
Badaling in Summer ↓

八达岭长城巨龙
Badaling sprawling like a huge dragon →

八达岭长城景观
Sceneries around Badaling ↓

43

嘉 峪 关 长 城
JIAYUGUAN

　　嘉峪关位于甘肃省嘉峪关市西。古称河西第一隘口，是著名丝绸之路的必经之路，亦为明代万里长城的西部终点。是现有长城诸多关城中保存最好的一座。

　　关城始建于明洪武五年（公元1372年）。因建于祁连山下的文殊山与黑山之间的嘉峪塬上而得名。关城呈梯形：西面城墙长166米，东面城墙长154米，南北两侧各长160米。城楼、敌台和垛口为砖包砌，其余为夯土建造。关城布局规整，城门上有三层高大门楼，关城四角建有角楼和角台。全关由内城、外城、瓮城、罗城及城壕组成。

　　嘉峪关建成后曾一度废置，明嘉靖十八年（公元1539年）重修加固，设重兵把守，清代后演变为检查过往商旅的关卡。

　　嘉峪关城建造精巧，楼阁飞檐凌空，雄伟壮观，亭台玲珑典雅，古朴华美，登楼远眺，戈壁风光，祁连雪景，尽收眼底。

Jiayuguan, the best preserved of all Great Wall passes, is in the west of Jiayuguan City, Gansu Province. It was known in ancient times as the first pass of Hexi and a key passageway of the Silk Road.

The castle began in 1372 (the 5th year of the Ming Hong Wu reign). It got its name for being located on the Jiayu Highland between the Wenshu and Heishan mountains at the foot of the Qilian Mountains. The pass is shaped like a trapezoid. The west wall is about 166 meters, the east wall 154 meters and the north and south are both 160 meters. The gatetower, watchtower and embrasures are brick and the rest is rammed earch. The pass has a good layout with a three-storied gatetower, 4 corner towers and consisting of an inner city wall, outer city wall, trenches, and fortifications with walls around them.

Once abandoned, Jiayuguan was rebuilt and reinforced in 1539 (the 18th year of the Ming Jiajing reign) and garrisoned. In the Qing Dynasty it became an office for checking merchants and travellers.

The architectural complex of the castle is magnificently exquisite. Its towers and pavilions have a classic beauty and grandeur with their roofs upturned at the end of the ridges. The castle commands fascinating views of the boundless Gobi Desert and the snowcapped Qilian Mountains.

关城外景
An outside view of the pass　↓

柔远楼
Rouyuan Tower ↑

将军府一角
A corner of a general's residence ↓

47

故宫外景
An outside view of the Palace Museum

故　宫
THE PALACE MUSEUM

故宫(又称紫禁城)位于北京市区中心。是明、清两代的皇宫。始建于明永乐四年(公元 1406 年),于永乐十八年(公元 1420 年)竣工。后又多次改建。是中国现存规模最大、最完整的古建筑群。东西宽 760 米,面积 72 万余平方米,据称有大小宫室 9999 间半。故宫建筑布局严格按照封建礼制,分为外朝、内廷两部分。外朝以太和殿、中和殿、保和殿为中心,殿体气势恢宏,庄严肃穆。内廷包括乾清宫、交泰殿、坤宁宫、御花园等。1911 年辛亥革命结束了清王朝统治,1924 年清王室出宫,1925 年成立故宫博物院。

Located in the center of Beijing the Palace Museum (also called the Forbidden City) was the imperial palace of the Ming and Qing dynasties. Construction of the palace started in 1406 (the 4th year of the Ming Yong Le reign) and ended in 1420 (the 18th year of the Yong Le reign). In the course of history it underwent many renovations and is now the largest and best preserved ancient architectural complex in China, covering an area of 720,000 square meters of land, and is 760 meters from east to west. The palace boasts of 9999.5 rooms. Its layout followed strict feudal code, with the palace ground divided into two main sections — the Front Palace and the Inner Palace. In the center of the Front Palace stand the Hall of Supreme Harmony, the Hall of Complete Harmony and the Hall of Preserving Harmony. The Inner Palace includes the Palace of Heavenly Purity, the Hall of Prosperity, the Hall of Earthly Peace and the Imperial Garden. The revolution in 1911 ended the rule of the Qing Dynasty and the imperial household was moved out in 1924. In 1925, the Palace Museum was set up.

太和殿　The Hall of Supreme Harmony

交泰殿
← Hall of Prosperity

储秀宫
Hall of Preserved Elegance ↓

御花园
Imperial Garden ↑

长春宫
Palace of Eternal Spring →

51

敦煌莫高窟全景
A panorama view of Mogao Grottoes

敦 煌 莫 高 窟
MOGAO GROTTOES
IN DUNHUANG

　　敦煌莫高窟位于甘肃省敦煌市鸣沙山东麓断崖上,又称千佛洞。莫高窟是世界上最大、内容最丰富和使用时间最长的佛教艺术宝库。自前秦建元二年(公元366年)开窟造像,历北魏、西魏、北周、隋、唐、五代、宋、西夏、元等时期,千余年从未停止。现保存下来的石窟492个,壁画面积达4.5万平方米,彩塑2400余身。

　　莫高窟绘画题材以佛像、经变、人物等为主,并反映了不同造窟时代的社会文化特征。更加弥足珍贵的是直观地将历代绘画造型的结构布局、人物造型、线描勾勒、敷彩设色等方面各个时期艺术风格及其传承演变以及中西艺术交融展现在人们面前。彩塑大者达33米,如巨型石胎泥塑弥勒像,小者仅10厘米。特别是魏唐时代的作品,更为人们誉为极品。

　　清光绪二十六年(公元1900年)藏经洞出土公元256年—1002年各种文书、绢画、刺绣等珍贵文物4500件,包括古藏文、梵文、回鹘文、于阗文、龟兹文等文字,被认为是世界上古代东方文化最伟大的发现。

Also called Caves of a Thousand Buddhas, the Mogao Grottoes are hewn in the steen cliffs of Mingsha Mountain of Dunhuang City, Gansu Province. The largest and richest Buddhist treasure trove in the world the Mogao Grottoes have been in use for the longest time. Construction never stopped for over a thousand years since 366 (the 2nd year of the Pre-Qin Jian Yuan reign) through Northern Wei, Western Wei, Northern Zhou, Sui, Tang, the Five Dynasties, Song, Western Xia and Yuan dynasties. The well-preserved 492 surviving caves have 45,000 square metres of murals and 2,400 painted statues.

The murals in the grottoes display Buddhas, tales of sutras, and human figures which reflect the cultural characteristics of the society during which the caves were hewn. They are valuable for they exhibit the composition and layout of paintings and sculptures through the dynasties, their figure delineation, line drawing, sketching and colouring, their heritage and transformation and their amalgamation with Western art. The painted statues vary in size, the largest being a 33-meter-high statue of a stone-bodied clay Maitreya Buddha and the smallest a mere 10 centimeters inheight. Even more remarkable are those done in the Wei and Tang dynasties.

In 1900 (the 26th year of the Qing Guang Xu reign), from the Sutra Cave were earthed 4,500 pieces of cultural relics dating from 250 to 1002 including embroideries, paintings on silk, priceless manuscripts and literature in ancient Tibetan, Sanskrit, Uygur, Yutian and Kuchah languages. This is the biggest find in the world about ancient oriental culture.

敦煌莫高窟九层楼 →
A nine-storey building at Mogao Grottoes, Dunhuang

彩塑一铺（盛唐）
Colored sculptures（Prosperous Tang）↓

彩塑菩萨（盛唐）
← A statue of Bodhisattva (Prosperous Tang)

国王与鹿（北魏）
The King and the Deer (Northern Wei) ↑

帝王出行图（初唐）
An Excursion of an Emperor (The beginning of Tang) ↓

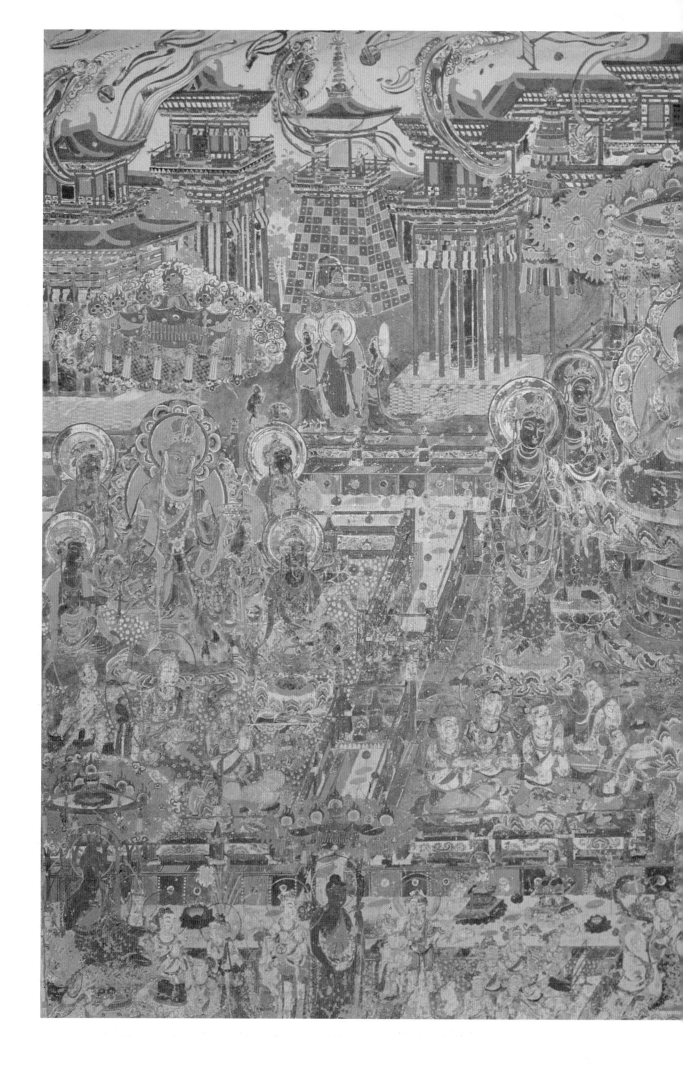

57

观无量寿经变图(盛唐)　A variation of *The Sutra of Contemplating Amitayus* (Prosperous Tang)

发掘中的秦兵马俑二号坑
Vault No.2 under excavation

秦始皇陵及兵马俑坑
QIN SHI HUANG'S MAUSOLEUM AND HIS TERRACOTTA ARMY

　　秦始皇陵及兵马俑坑,位于陕西省西安市临潼县东骊山北麓。建于公元前 246 年至公元前 208 年,历时 39 年,是中国历史上第一个规模比较完善的帝王陵寝,现存陵冢高 76 米,陵园布置仿秦都咸阳,分内外两城,内城周长 2.5 公里,外城周长 6.3 公里。陵冢位于内城西南,坐西面东。

　　兵马俑坑是秦始皇陵东侧的一组大型陪葬坑,1974 年发现,已发掘的三个俑坑,出土仿真人真马大小的陶制兵马俑约 8000 件。陶俑神情生动,形象准确,轩昂肃穆;陶马造型逼真,刻划精致自然。兵马俑是秦国强大军队的缩影,布局排列如军阵,气势凛然。

　　兵俑所持武器均为实用兵器,一、二、三号坑共出土万余件。其中一把青铜剑,长 90 厘米,剑身表面经过铬化处理,虽历经两千余年,仍毫无锈蚀。陵冢两侧出土的

约为实物四分之一大小的铜车马更被誉为"青铜之冠",堪称人类冶金史上的奇迹,是中华民族的瑰宝。

　　被誉为"世界奇迹"的兵马俑坑正在进一步发掘,更丰富多彩的地下宝藏即将同世人见面。

　　Located in the north of Mount Lishan, Lintong County, Xi'an, Shaanxi Province are the mausoleum of Qin Shi Huang, the first emperor of Qin, and his buried terracotta soldiers. The building of the tomb started in 246 BC and lasted 39 years until 208 BC. It is the first imperial mausoleum of dimensions in Chinese history. Today the mound still stands 76 meters high. The layout of its grounds followed that of Xianyang, the capital of Qin, with inner and outer walls. The circumference of the inner wall is 2.5 kilometers, that of the outer wall is 6.3 kilometers. The mausoleum sits in the southwest of the inner city, facing east.

To the east of the mausoleum lies the terracotta army buried with Qin Shi Huang. Discovered in 1974, 8,000 life-size terracotta warriors and horses were found in three vaults. The well modelled and proportioned warriors are strong and firm in appearance. The horses are highly realistic, the delineation natural and exquisite. They are arranged in military formation, demonstrating the power of Qin Shi Huang's army.

The warriors carry real weapons. Over ten thousand weapons are unearthed from the three vaults. The chromized blade of one 90-cm-long bronze sword is free of rust after being buried for two thousand years. Chariots and horses, one fourth of the original sizes, are unearthed at the wings of the mausoleum and known as the "crown of bronzes". They are a miracle in the history of metallurgy and a treasure of the Chinese people.

More excavations are being done to the buried army known as a "wonder of the world" and more treasures are expected to be found.

高级军吏俑
A terracotta figure of an officer ↑

一号坑秦兵马俑内景
Detail of Vault No. 1 ↓

秦兵马俑二号坑外景
Outside view of Vault No. 2 ↑

二号坑出土的跪射俑
← Excavation of a kneeling archer
in Vault No. 2

60

秦始皇帝陵
Qin Shi Huang's tomb ↑

秦陵铜车马
Bronze chariot and horses in Qin Shi Huang's Mausoleum ↓

周口店全景
A panorama view of Zhoukoudian

周口店北京人遗址
ZHOUKOUDIAN—HOME OF PEKING MAN

　　周口店北京人遗址位于北京市房山区周口店龙骨山。因本世纪二十年代出土了较为完整的北京猿人化石而闻名于世,尤其是 1929 年发现了第一具北京人头盖骨,从而为北京人的存在提供了坚实的基础,成为古人类研究史上的里程碑。到目前为止,出土的人类化石包括 6 件头盖骨、15 件下颌骨、157 枚牙齿及大量骨骼碎块,代表约 40 个北京猿人个体。为研究人类早期的生物学演化及早期文化的发展提供了实物依据。

　　根据对文化沉积物的研究,北京人生活在距今 70 万年至 20 万年之间。北京人的平均脑量达 1088 毫升(现代人脑量为 1400),据推算北京人身高为 156 厘米(男),150 厘米(女)。北京人属石器时代,加工石器的方法主要为锤击法,其次为砸击法,偶见砧击法。北京人还是最早使用火的古人类,并能捕猎大型动物。北京人的寿命较短,据统计,68.2% 死于 14 岁前,超过 50 岁的不足 4.5%。

　　在龙骨山顶部于 1930 年发掘出生活于 2 万年前后的古人类化石,并命名为"山顶洞人"。1973 年又发现介于二者年代之间的"新洞人",表明北京人的延续和发展。

The remains of the home of Peking Man is located on Dragon Bone Hill near the town of Zhoukoudian, Fanshan District, Beijing (Peking). The place became world renowned since the discovery of a well-preserved fossil of a Peking Man in the 20s and particularly when the first skull of a Peking Man was found in 1929. These discoveries are solid proofs of the existence of Peking Man, a milestone in the history of the study of paleoanthropology. Unearthed fossil remains in Zhoukoudian include 6 skulls, 15 mandibles, 157 teeth and countless fragmented bones belonging to 40 individual Peking Men, providing important material for the studies of the early biological evolution of human beings and the development of culture in the early stage.

The study of cultural sediments show that Peking Man lived from 7 to 2 hundred thousand years ago. The average weight of Peking Man's brains is 1,088 ml. (That of modern man is 1,400 ml.) The calculated height of Peking Man is 156 cm. That of Peking

Woman is 150 cm. They lived in the Stone Age, making stone implements by hammering, pounding and in some rare cases striking on anvils. Fire was first used by Peking Man who hunted large animals too. Peking Man did not live long — 68.2% died before 14. Those who lived over 50 were less than 4.5%.

In 1930 fossils of Upper Cave Man who lived 20 thousand years ago were found on the top of Dragon Bone Hill. In 1973 New Cave Man who lived between the periods of the existance of Peking Man and Upper Cave Man was discovered, showing a continuation and development of Peking Man.

北京人遗址内景
An inside view of Peking Man's cave →

山顶洞人遗址外景
An outer view of a cave of Upper Cave Man ↓

北京人塑像
A sculpture of Peking Man

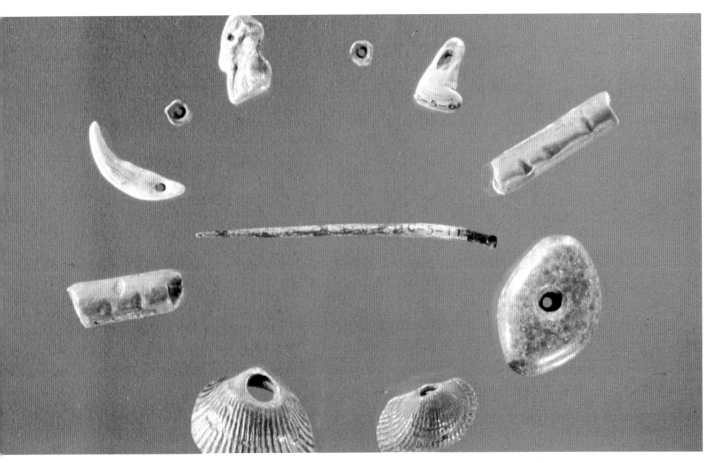

山顶洞人装饰物
Ornaments of Upper Cave Man.　↑

北京人第一具完整的头盖骨
The first well-preserve skull-cap of Peking Man.　↓

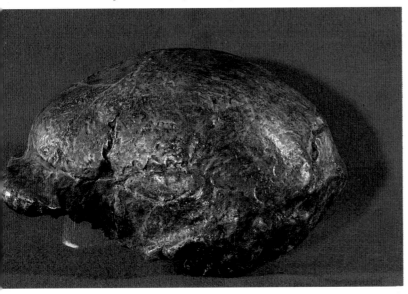

北京人石器
A stone implement of Peking Man.　↑

泰山风景名胜区
MOUNT TAISHAN

泰山位于山东省中部,跨越泰安、济南两市。总面积 250 平方公里,古称岱山,春秋时改称泰山,被尊为东岳。其山势磅礴雄伟,峰峦突兀峻拔,景色壮丽,中国历代帝王秦始皇、汉武帝、唐玄宗、清帝乾隆等均曾到泰山封禅,历代七十二君主到此祭告天地。

泰山拥有丰富的自然遗产。景区内自古命名的山峰 112 座,崖岭 98 座,岩洞 18 处,奇石 58 块,溪谷 102 条,潭池瀑布 56 处,山泉 64 处,共有植物 144 科,989 种,植被覆盖率为 79.9%。泰山风景区拥有连续数千年的历史文化遗产。现有古建筑群 22 处,古遗址 97 处,历代碑碣 819 块,历代刻石 1800 余处,为研究中国古代历史、书法等提供了重要而丰富的实物资料。主要景观包括天贶殿、南天门、碧霞祠、日观峰、经石峪、黑龙潭等。泰山是一座具有美学、科学和历史文化价值的名山,圣山。

Mount Taishan is located in the center of Shandong Province spanning the cities of Taian and Jinan, extending for a total area of 250 kilometers. It was known in ancient times as Daishan and revered as the East Sacred Mountain. Mount Taishan is a symbol of loftiness and grandeun with abruptly rising majestic peaks and crests. Its sceneries are spectacular. Many Chinese emperors including Qin Shi Huang, Wu Di of Han, Xuan Zong of Tang and Qian Long of Qing held grand sacrificial ceremonies on its summit. All through the dynasties 72 emperors had come here to offer sacrifices to heaven and earth.

Mount Taishan boasts of a wealth of natural legacies. A large number of scenic spots were given names since ancient times. They include 112 peaks, 98 precipitous ridges, 18 rock caves, 58 oddshaped rocks, 102 streams and valleys, 56 pools and waterfalls, 64 springs. It has 989 species of plants falling into 114 families, and a vegetation coverage of 79.9 percent. With cultural legacies handing down through thousands of years, the scenic area houses 22 groups of ancient architectures, 97 ancient remains, 819 commemorative stone tablets and 1,800 inscribed rocks. They are a natural museum for the study of ancient Chinese History and calligraphy. Its main sites of interest include Hall of Heavenly Blessing, South Gate to Heaven, Azure Cloud Temple, Sun Watching Peak, Sutra Rock Valley and Black Dragon Pool. Mount Taishan is a famed Sacred Mountain valuable in aesthetics, science and cultural history.

五岳独尊
First of the Five Sacred Mountains →

中天门
Halfway Gate to Heaven ↓

泰山日出 Sunrise on Mt. Taishan

姊妹松
Sister Pine Trees ↑

十八盘
← The Eighteen Mountain Bends

碧霞祠
Azure Cloud Temple →

71

黄山位于安徽省南部,跨歙、黟、太平、休宁四县,秦时称黟山,唐天宝六年(公元747年)改称黄山。景区面积154平方公里,是一座综合峰、石、松、云、泉等各种罕见景观的风景名胜区。

黄山素以奇松、怪石、云海、温泉"四绝"著称于世,罕见的地质结构,奇特的峰林地貌,是黄山地貌景观的主要特色。景区内独特的花岗岩峰林,遍布峰壑、千姿百态的黄山松,惟妙惟肖的怪石,变幻莫测的云海,构成了黄山静中有动、动中有静的巨幅画卷。黄山有丰富的原生植物种质资源和野生动物资源。景区内森林覆盖率83.4%,原生种质植物203科、1452种。黄山还具有丰富的文化遗产。明代著名地理学家徐霞客两游黄山,赞曰:"薄海内外无如徽之黄山,登黄山天下无山,观止矣!"后人述之为:"五岳归来不看山,黄山归来不看岳。"

Huangshan Mountain is located in the south of Anhui Province, Spanning She, Yi, Taiping and Xiuning counties. It was called Yishan Mountain in the Qin Dynesty and acquired its present name Huangshan Mountain in 747 (the 6th year of the Tang Tianbao reign). Its scenic area, covering 154 square kilometers of land, encompasses fascinating peaks, rocks, pines, clouds, springs and other rare scenes.

Huangshan Mountain is celebrated for having four wonderful mountain scenes: odd-shaped pines, bizarre rocks, cloud seas and hot springs. Rare geological formation and spectacular clusters of peaks are the natural characteristics of Huangshan Mountain. In the scenic area, unique granite peaks dotting the summits and cliffs; ancient pines stretching their branches in every posture, bizarre rocks with strong resemblances to whatever in your imagination; and the seas of cloud so full of unpredictable changes — they combine to unfold a large scroll of Huangshan Mountain showing movement in tranquility and vice versa. Huangshan Mountain houses rich resources of protophyte and wild animals. The scenic area has a forest coverage of 83.4% and 1,452 species of protophytes falling into 203 families. Huangshan Mountain has a wealth of cultural heritage too. On his second visit to Huangshan Xu Xiake, noted traveller and geographer of the Ming Dynasty, exclaimed: "Huangshan Mountain in Anhui has no equal. Once on top, one finds no other match. This is the acme!" Later man made the following statement: "One visits no mountains after the Five Sacred Mountains. And after Huangshan, one has no eye for the Five Sacred Mountains."

北海宾馆
Beihai Hotel

黄山云海
Cloud seas on Huangshan Mountain ↑

飞来石　Rock Which Flew Here ↑

迎客松
Guest-Welcoming Pine ↑

黄山峰林
← Peak forest on Huangshan Mountain

76

猴子观海 "Monkeys" Watching the Sea ↑

天子山御笔峰
Peak of Imperial Writing Brush on Tianzi Mountain

武陵源风景名胜区
WULINGYUAN SCENIC AREA

武陵源风景名胜区位于湖南省张家界市。总面积264平方公里,由张家界国家森林公园、索溪峪和天子山等三大景区组成。主要景观为石英砂岩峰林地貌,境内共有3103座奇峰,姿态万千,蔚为壮观。加之沟壑纵横,溪涧密布,森林茂密,人迹罕至,森林覆盖率85%,植被覆盖率99%,中、高等植物3000余种,乔木树种700余种,可供观赏园林花卉多达450种。陆生脊椎动物50科116种。区内地下溶洞串珠贯玉,已开发的黄龙洞初探长度达11公里。武陵源以奇峰、怪石、幽谷、秀水、溶洞"五绝"而闻名于世。

Located at Zhangjiajie City, Hunan Province and covering 264 square kilometers of land the Wulingyuan Scenic Area emcompasses the Zhangjiajie National Forest Park, Suoxiyu and Tianzishan Nature Reserves. The spectacular quartz-sandstone formation is noted for its clusters of peaks, 3,103 in number, in all wonderful shapes. Crisscrossed by valleys, ravines and streams, the densely wooded forests are untraversed by men. Wulingyuan has a forest coverage of 85% and a vegetation coverage of 99%. It houses over 3,000 species of high- and middle-level plants, 700 arbor species, 450 species of ornamental flowers, and 116 species of terrestrial vertebrates falling into 50 families. The chain of underground karst caves stretches like a string of pearls. The first exploration of Yellow Dragon Cave reveals a length of 11 kilometers. Wulingyuan is known in the world with the following five outstanding features — spetacular peaks, unique rocks, secluded vallays, serene waters, and karst caves.

仙女献花　Goddess Presenting Flowers　↑

天子山云海　A sea of clouds on Tianzi Mountain　↓

宝峰湖
Baofeng Lake ↑

雪 景
A scene of snow →

索溪峪
Suoxiyu Nature Reserve ↓

九寨沟风景名胜区
JIUZHAIGOU SCENIC AREA

  九寨沟风景名胜区位于四川省阿坝藏族羌族自治州南坪县境内,风景区面积 720 平方公里。九寨沟集湖、瀑、滩、流、雪峰、森林、藏族风情为一体。主景区位于全长 60 多公里的山谷中。谷中有 108 个湖泊,山顶为一长度 7000 米,宽数百米的"长海",湖水中随处可见自然倒下的古树,树枝上包裹碳酸钙华,阳光折射之下五彩缤纷。被形象地称为五彩湖。自长海以下,各湖泊之间形成了数十个大小瀑布,其中尤以诸日那瀑布为最。九寨沟风景区动植物资源丰富,自然分布原生植物 2576 种,由于其地处亚热带与温带交会处,使得景区内既有亚热带植物,又有适合温带生长的油松、华山松等,形成植物垂直带谱。九寨沟有脊椎动物 170 种,鸟类 141 种,其中含国家一类保护动物大熊猫、牛羚、金丝猴,二类保护动物 4 种及三类保护动物 9 种。

Jiuzhaigou Scenic Area, lying in Nanping County of Tibetan and Qiang Autonomous Prefecture of Aba in Sichuan Province, covers 720 square kilometers of land. It encompasses lakes, waterfalls, shoals, streams, snow-capped mountains, forests as well as Tibetan villages. Most of the sceneries stretch along a valley over 60 kilometers long. There are 108 lakes in the valley. The summit is a "long sea" 7,000 meters in length and hundreds of meters in width. Ancient trees, toppled by Nature, strew the water. Covered by travertine carbonate the tree branches glitter in many colors in the rays of the sun. Thus the lake is also called Colorful Lake. A breathtaking spectacle is the dozens of rushing waterfalls cascading between the lakes. The Nuorina Waterfall in the center of the Yellow Dragon Raving is most magnificent. Jiuzhaigou Scenic Area has a rich resources of flora and fauna and houses, 2,576 species of protophites. Being at the juncture of the subtropical and the temperate Zones, the scenic area houses trees suited to both zones such as Chinese tallow tree (Sapium sebiferum), and Chinese pine (Pinus tabulaeformis), forming a vertical flora zonation. The place houses 170 species of vertebrates and 141 species of birds including Giant Panda, gnu, and Golden Monkey, all at the first level of national protection, 4 species of animals at the secondary level of protection, and 9 species of animals at the tertiary level of protection.

翠 湖
Emerald Lake　↑

五彩湖
Colorful Lake　↓

争艳池
Pool of Vying for Beauty

黄龙风景名胜区
YELLOW DRAGON SCENIC AREA

　　黄龙风景名胜区位于四川省阿坝藏族羌族自治州松潘县境内。面积700平方公里。主要景观集中于长约3.6公里的黄龙沟,沟内遍布碳酸钙华沉积,并呈梯田状排列,仿佛是一条金色巨龙,并伴有雪山、瀑布、原始森林、峡谷等景观。黄龙风景名胜区既以独特的岩溶景观著称于世,也以丰富的动植物资源享誉人间。从黄龙沟底部(海拔2000米)到山顶(海拔3800米)依次出现亚热带常绿与落叶阔叶混交林、针叶阔叶混交林、亚高山针叶林、高山灌丛草甸等。包括大熊猫、金丝猴在内的10余种珍贵动物徜徉其间,使黄龙景区的特殊岩溶地貌与珍稀动植物资源相互交织,浑然天成。以其雄、峻、奇、野风景特色,享有"世界奇观"、"人间瑶池"的美誉。

Located in Songpan County of Tibetan and Qiang Autonomous Prefecture of Aba in Sichuan Province, Yellow Dragon Scenic Area covers 700 square kilometers of land. Its main sights of interest are grouped in the 3.6 kilometer-long Yellow Dragon Ravine which is covered with layers of sedimentary travertine carbonate like terraced fields, resembling a huge yellow dragon. Other sceneries include snow-capped mountains, watefalls, virgin forests and canyons. Apart from its unique karst landform, Yellow Dragon Scenic Area is also known for its rich resources of flora and fauna. From the bottom of Yellow Dragon Ravine (2,000 meters above sea level) to the mountain top (3,800 meters above sea level) exist in sequence subtropical evergreen trees mingled with deciduous broadleaf trees, conniferous and broadleaf mingled forests, conniferous orohylile, and coryphile. Sauntering among these forests are a dozen rare animal species including Giant Panda and Golden Monkey. The karst landform complimented by rare flora and fauna resources presents a heavenly scene. And the majestic, precipitous, grotesque and primeval sceneries win Yellow Dragon Scenic Area many titles including "the world's marvellous scenery" and "immortals' abode on earth".

人间仙境
Paradise on Earth ↑

明镜倒影
Reflections in the Mirror Lake ↓

普宁寺全景
Puning Temple

承德避暑山庄及周围寺庙
CHENGDE MOUNTAIN RESORT AND TEMPLES AROUND IT

承德避暑山庄及周围寺庙位于河北省承德市。康熙四十二年(公元1703年)开始建避暑山庄,至乾隆五十七年(公元1792年)竣工,历经89年。既具北方之雄,更兼南方之秀,又因地距北京仅250公里,"奏章朝发夕至,综理万机,与宫中无异",故康、乾历代皇帝每年三月三至九月九,均率嫔妃和大臣来此,并进行议论朝政、部落首领朝拜和接见外国使者的活动,从而使承德成为清代第二政治中心。山庄内主要包括:澹泊敬诚殿,全部为楠木建造,整座宫殿不施油彩,极富特色;文津阁,专为存放《四库全书》建造,现存于北京图书馆的四库全书便是在这里保存下来的,以及金山寺、烟雨楼、如意洲等等。

周围寺庙指分布于避暑山庄的北部和东部山麓的12座喇嘛寺庙,是清王朝联络各族王公贵族,实现民族团结政策的体现。现存主要庙宇有:普宁寺、普乐寺、须弥福寿之庙、普陀宗乘之庙、安远庙和殊像寺。

The Mountain Resort for Escaping the Heat and the temples around it are located in Chengde City, Hebei Province. Its construction lasted 89 years from 1703 (the 42nd year of the Qing Kang Xi reign) to 1792 (the 57th year of the Qing Qian Long reign). The various buildings possess characteristics of the scenery of both north and south China — majesty and elegance. Being but 250 kilometers from Beijing and that documents could arrive from one place to the other the same day, Kang Xi, Qian Long and emperors after them would come here with their harem and ministers every year from the third day of the third lunar month to the ninth day of the ninth month. The emperors continued to discuss court affairs and received the nobility of China's various nationalities and foreign envoys here and it became the second political center of the Qing Dynasty. The main hall called Danpojingcheng built entirely of a fine-grained hardwood — *nanmu* — is austere and unadorned. Wenjin Pavilion is built to house the "Complete Works of the Four Treasures" compiled in the Qing Dynasty. This copy is now in the collection of the National Library of China. Also in the grounds are Jinshan Temple, Temple of Smoke and Rain and Ruyi Oasis.

Outside the enclosure of the Mountain Resort 12 lama temples dot the slopes in the north and in the east. They manifest the Qing policy of uniting the

避暑山庄湖区鸟瞰
A bird's -eye view of the
lake district of Chengde
Mountain Resort →

普陀宗乘之庙
Putuozongsheng Temple ↓

nationalities and befriending their nobility. The
temples that remain to this day include Puning, Pule,
Xumifushou, Putuozongsheng, Anyuan and
Shuxiang.

普宁寺千手千眼观音菩萨塑像
The Thousand-handed and Thousand-
eyed Goddess of Mercy in Puning Temple →

孔庙大成殿
Hall of Great Achievements in Confucius Temple

曲阜孔庙、孔府、孔林
CONFUCIUS TEMPLE, RESIDENCE AND CONFUCIAN WOODS

曲阜孔庙、孔府、孔林位于山东省曲阜市,是中国历代纪念孔子,推崇儒学的表征,以丰厚的文化积淀、悠久历史、宏大规模、丰富文物珍藏,以及科学艺术价值而著称。

孔庙位于曲阜城的中央。据史料记载,在孔子辞世的第二年(公元前478年)鲁哀公将孔子旧居改建为祭祀孔子的庙宇。经历代重建扩修,明代形成了现有规模。前后九进院落,占地面积14万平方米,庙内共有殿阁亭堂门坊100余座。孔庙内有孔子讲学的杏坛、手植桧,存有历代碑刻1000余块。

孔府本名衍圣公府。位于孔庙东侧,为孔子嫡长孙的衙署。汉高祖刘邦曾以太牢之礼祭孔子墓并封孔子九世孙世袭为奉祀君,代表国家祭祀孔子。后历代不断加封,至宋代封为衍圣公。明洪武十年建立独立的衍圣公府。现有楼、房、厅、堂480余间,前为官衙,后为内宅。府内存有著名的孔府档案和大量文物。

孔林位于曲阜北,为孔子及其后裔的家族墓地。孔子卒于鲁哀公十六年(公元前479年)四月已丑,葬鲁城北泗上。其后代从冢而葬,形成今天的孔林。从子贡为孔子庐墓植树起,孔林内古树已达万余株。历代墓葬10余万座,碑刻4000余通,桃花扇作者著名文学家孔尚任的墓葬亦在此。

The Temple of Confucius, the Confucius Family Mansion and the Confucian Woods are located in the city of Qufu, Shandong Province. They symbolize the Chinese people's remembrance of Confucius throughout the ages, and their respect to Confucianism. They are known for their cultural significance, agelong history, considerable scale, rich collection of relics and their scientific and artistic value.

According to historical records, in 478 BC, the year after Confucius' death, Lord Ai of the State of Lu had Confucius' house in the center of Qufu altered into a temple in commemoration of the sage.

After many rebuilds and expansions, it reached its present scale in the Ming Dynasty. Covering 140,000 square meters of land it has over a hundred halls, towers, pavilions and other buildings clustering around 9 courtyards. There are also the Apricot Altar where Confucius had his school, the famous cypress and over a thousand stone tablets.

To the east of the temple is Confucius' house. It was once Confucius' eldest grandson's *yamen* and named Lord Yansheng's Residence. During the Han Dynasty Emperor Gao Zu, named Liu Bang, made offerings at Confucius' tomb in the highest degree. The emperor also conferred on Confucius' ninth generation direct grandson and his sons after him an official post supervising sacrifices to Confucius on behalf of the country. In the course of history, many titles were conferred on Confucius and his

孔庙杏坛
Apricot Altar in Confucius Temple.　→

孔庙大成殿龙柱
Dragon columns of Hall of Great
Achievements in Confucius Temple.　↓

孔府大门内景
← A view of the gate of Confucius residence.

孔府花园
Garden in Confucius Residence. ↓

孔　府
Confucius Residence. ↑

descendants. The title of Yansheng was given to his
descendant in the Song Dynasty. In the 10th year of
the Ming Hong Wu reign an independent Residence
of Lord Yansheng was set up, with the *yamen* in the
front and the domestic household at the back. It has
480 rooms and houses many files and relics.

Located in the north of Qufu is the Confucian
Woods where the tombs of Confucius and most of
his descendants are to be found. After Confucius'
death in April 479 BC, (the 16th year of Lord Ai of
Lu), his descendants buried with him and the place
gradually grew into a cemetery with over 100,000
tombs and 4,000 steles. Zi Gong, Confucius'
desciple, started planting trees at Confucius' tomb
and now there are over 10,000 trees in the woods.
Kong Shangren, well-known *literatus* and author of
the "Peach Blossom Fan", was buried here too.

孔府红尊轩内景
Inside view of Red Sepal Pavilion in →
Confucius Residence.

93

孔子墓
Tomb of Confucius. ↑

孔子之孙孔伋墓
Tomb of Kong Ji
(confucius' Grandson)
in Confucian Woods.　→

孔林万古长春坊
Archway of Even-Lasting
Spring in Confucian
Woods.　↓

南岩宫
South Rock Palace

武当山古建筑群
ANCIENT ARCHITECTURE IN WUDANG MOUNTAIN

　　武当山,旧称太和山、仙石山。位于湖北省丹江口市。主峰(天柱峰)海拔 1612 米,武当山有七十二峰、三十六岩、二十四涧、三潭、九井、十池等胜境,众多奇峰异景环绕天柱峰,形成"万山来朝"的独特风格。武当山植被完整,植物资源丰富,仅明代药学家李时珍所著《本草纲目》中记载的 1800 种中草药有 600 种以上选自武当山。故武当山有"天然药库"之称。

　　武当山风景区自然景观与人文景观融为一体,据传,周代已开始有人在此结茅修炼,唐贞观年间(公元 627 至 649 年)建五龙祠,后历代均有修建。明成祖朱棣崇奉道教,于永乐十年(公元 1412 年)敕建宫观达33 处,至永乐二十一年(公元 1423 年)最后完工,从而形成了九宫、九观、七十二岩庙、三十六庵堂的大型建筑群,总面积达 160 万平方米的规模。尤其是主峰绝顶的金殿,除殿基为花岗岩外,均为精铜所铸,并经铆榫而成。殿内"真武"坐像是我国古代铜铸艺术的精品。

　　武当山武术为内家拳之源流,相传为张三丰所创。武当山的道教音乐也是中华音乐的活化石。

　　Also called Taihe Mountain and Xianshi Mountain, the Wudang Mountain is located in Danjiangkou City, Hubei Province. Its main peak, Tianzhu Peah, is 1612 meters above sea level. Clustering around it are numerous strikingly outstanding peaks and exotic sceneries as if "ten thousands peaks are paying their homage". Its scenic spots include 72 peaks, 36 rocky cliffs, 24 streams, 3 pools, 9 wells, and 10 lakes. Wudang Mountain, well-covered with vegetation, has a rich resources of plants; 600 of the 1,800 medicinal herbs recorded in "Compendium of Materia Medica" compiled by the

Ming Dynasty pharmacist Li Shizhen are chosen from Wudang Mountain. Therefore the mountain is also known as a "natural herbary".

Man-made sceneries on Wudang Mountain compliment natural ones. Legend has it that as early as the Zhou Dynasty people began to build thatched huts here to practise Buddhism. A Five-Dragon Temple was built during the Tang Zhen Guan reign (627-649) and renovations were done in later dynasties. Being a Daoist, Emperor Cheng Zu of the Ming Dynasty started building 33 halls and monasteries in 1412 (the 10th year of the Yong Le reign). The construction was finally finished in 1423 (the 21st year of the Ming Yong Le reign). The large architectural complex includes 9 halls, 9 monasteries, 72 temples and 36 nunneries with a total floor space of 1.6 million square meters. A refined copper hall perches on a granite foundation on the main peak. A sitting stature of God Zhenwu in the hall built with rivets and tenons is an exquisite example of ancient Chinese art of copper casting.

Wudang Mountain is the source of the Kung Fu of the internal school boxing created by Zhang Sanfeng. The Daoist music in the mountain is also a living fossil of the music of China.

圣 牌
Sacred Tablet ↑

武当山进山大门
The gate leading into Mount Wudang ↓

紫霄宫
← Purple Cloud Palace

复真观
Truth-Returning Nunnery ↓

铜铸真武神像
Bronze statue of God Zhenwu ↑

金　殿
Golden Hall　↑

剑河桥
← Sword River Bridge

100

太和宫
Palace of Supreme Harmony ↑

布达拉宫
Potala Palace

布 达 拉 宫
POTALA PALACE OF LHASA

布达拉宫位于西藏自治区拉萨市布达拉山（原名红山）上，始建于公元7世纪，是吐蕃赞普松赞干布为迎娶文成公主所建。后历世多有修筑。清顺治二年（公元1645年）达赖五世被清政府封为西藏地方政教首领，开始扩建，始具有今天的规模。达赖五世于清顺治十年（公元1653年）由哲蚌寺移驻布达拉宫，从此，布达拉宫成为西藏地方政治中心，布达拉山是梵语（古印度语）的音译，即普陀山的意思。

布达拉宫依山而建，主要包括宫殿、佛堂、灵塔殿，以及南面广场和北面广场、龙王潭。主楼共13层，高110余米，东西长360余米，八座祭堂拱卫主殿，供奉佛像数万尊。7世纪保存下来的法王修行洞内尚存松赞干布和文成公主塑像。历代达赖灵塔殿内的灵塔建筑精美，尤其是五世达赖灵塔外部全部用金皮包裹，镶嵌大量珍贵珠宝，制作备极精美。钦厦是清朝驻藏大臣为达赖主持坐床、亲政仪式之处。

布达拉宫依山垒砌，殿厦连接，相互呼应，整个建筑群蔚为壮观，充分体现了以藏族为主，汉、蒙古、满等各族能工巧匠的高超技艺和藏族建筑艺术的伟大成就。

Potala Palace, standing on top a cliff in Lhasa, capital of the Tibet Autonomous Region, started building in the 7th century by King Songtsan Gambo for his bride the Han nationality Princess Wen Cheng. In 1645 (the 2nd year of the Qing Shun Zhi reign) when the Fifth Dalai Lama was made political and religious leader of Tibet by the Qing government, reconstruction and expansion of the Palace were carried out until it reached the present scale. The Fifth Dalai Lama began living there in 1653 (the 10th year of Shun Zhi) and since then Potala Palace has become Tibet's political center. "Potala" is the Sanskrit pronounciation of "Buddha's Mountain".

Built against the slope of a hill Potala Palace consists of halls, the main building, the worshipping hall and the Hall of Stupas, an open square in the south and also in the north, and a Dragon King's Pool etc. Clustering around the main building, which is 110 meters high and 360 meters wide from east to west, are 8 sacrificial halls housing tens of thousands of buddist statues. In the Cave where the King Dharma Practises Buddism built in the 7th century are statues of King Songtsan Gambo

布达拉宫的主尊佛
帕巴鲁格夏日佛
Statue of Sacred
Avalokitesvara
in Potala Palace →

and Princess Wen Cheng. The stupas of the Dalai Lamas are extremely exquisite, particularly that of the Fifth Dalai Lama's which is covered with gold leaf and studled with jade and precious stones. The East Main Hall was the place where ceremonies for the assumptions of office by the Dalai Lamas were presided over by ministers from the Qing Dynasty central government.

The splendour of the Potala Palace is a great achievement of Tibetan architectural art which also amalgamates the skills of artisans of the Han, Mongolian and Manchu nationalities.

一山飞峙大江边
A Mountain Towering over the Yangtze

庐山风景名胜区
MOUNT LUSHAN

庐山,位于江西省北部,北濒长江,东南临鄱阳湖。自然风光奇特秀丽。"匡庐奇秀甲天下山。"方圆302平方公里的风景区内,有16个大自然奇观,474处景点。171座山峰逶迤相连,峰峦叠嶂。

庐山奇伟幽险、瀑飞泉鸣;云蒸雾涌,气象万千。3000余种植物分布在云山锦谷,苍翠斑斓、争奇竞妍。独特的第四纪冰川遗迹,使其平添几分神秘色彩。山麓的鄱阳湖候鸟多达百万,世界上最大鹤群在水天之间翩翩起舞,构成了鹤飞千点的世界奇观。

庐山,历史文化悠久丰厚。早在远古时期,庐山就曾出现我们祖先的遗迹。西汉历史学家司马迁南登庐山,将庐山之名载入《史记》至今已有2000多年。白鹿洞书院列我国古代四大书院之首,在中国教育史上享有盛誉。东晋高僧建造的东林寺,是佛教净土宗的发源地。历史上先后有1500多位名人登庐山,为庐山留下了4000余首诗词、900余处摩崖石刻和浩如烟海的著作、画卷及书法作品。现存的600余栋风格迥异、造型别致的别墅,反映了18个不同国家和民族的文化底蕴。

Mount Lushan is located in the north of Jiangxi Province, with the Changjiang River flowing by just in the north and the Poyang Lake lying in the southeast. Known as "the most beautiful mountain under heaven" its scenic area covers 302 square kilometers of land, including 16 natural wonders, 474 scenic spots and 171 peaks standing on rolling mountain ranges.

Waterfalls roaring like thunder cascade down precipitous cliffs and gurgling streams meander through serene nooks. Clouds and vapor float and wrap the scenery in a blanket of mist. In the misty slopes and valleys over three thousand species of plants produce a world of green bespeckled with a myrial colors while the remains of the quaternary glaciers add an air of mystery to the beauty of the mountain. A million migrant birds soar above the waters of the Poyang Lake, the largest group of cranes in the world dance between heaven and water. A really wonderful sight!

Mount Lushan has a very long cultural history. There were traces of our ancestors as early as remote antiquity. Over two thousand years ago Qian Sima, historian of Western Han Dynasty, recorded the mountain in his "Records of the Historian". White Deer Cave Academy, the most important of the four ancient academies of China, enjoys fame in the history of Chinese education. East Forest Monastery, constructed by an eminent monk in Eastern Jin (317-420), is the place where the Pure Land Sect of Buddhism originated. More than 1,500 famous men have ascended Mount Lushan at different times in history, leaving behind 4,000 poems, 900 inscriptions on rocky cliffs, and countless paintings, caligraphy, and books. The surviving 600 villas built in unique styles and shapes exhibit the culture of 18 countries and nations.

庐山松
Lushan Pine ↑

如琴湖之春
Spring over Ruqin Lake ↓

白鹿洞书院
White Deer Cave Academy in Mt. Lushan — one
of the four oldest academy of China

湖畔别墅
Villas by the Lake

小天池云雾
Foggy Small
Heavenly Pool
→

三叠泉瀑布
Three Cascades
Waterfall
←

美庐别墅　↑
Meilu Villa

芦林冰窖　↓
Ice-Kiln of Lulin — quatenary glacial remains

峨眉秋色
Autumn in Mount Emei

峨眉山——乐山大佛
风景名胜区

MOUNT EMEI AND THE GIANT BUDDHA OF LESHAN

峨眉山位于四川省峨眉山市,是集自然风光与佛教文化为一体的山岳型风景名胜区。峨眉山以其特殊的地理位置、雄秀神奇的自然景观、典型的地质地貌、保护完好的生态环境而著称,特别是地处世界生物区系的结合和过渡地带,拥有高等植物3200多种和动物2300多钟,古老珍稀物种繁多,具有明显的区域特点。海拔3077米的主峰金顶,可观日出、云海、佛光、晚霞四大奇观。洗象池、九老洞、洪椿坪是峨眉山腹心之地,秀色所在,花木繁茂,绿树常荫。近两千多年来,创造和积累了以佛教为主要特征的丰富文化遗产。万年寺的无梁砖殿建筑风格别致,殿内供奉的普贤铜佛像,铸造于公元980年,重62吨,高7.85米,为全国重点文物。报国寺为峨眉山佛事活动的主坛场。伏虎寺环

境幽静,寺周古楠参天,为山中最大寺院。峨眉山具有很高的历史、美学、科研、科普和游览观光价值。

乐山大佛风景区与峨眉山遥遥相对。乐山大佛风景区以精粹的文化遗产和丰富的自然遗产有机结合为特色,以"极世界佛像之大"的乐山大佛著称于世。景区面积2.5平方公里,以唐代摩崖造像乐山大佛为中心,有秦蜀守李冰开凿的离堆——乌尤山、汉代崖墓群、唐宋佛像、宝塔、寺庙、明清建筑等多处文物古迹。享誉中外的通高71米的乐山大佛,依崖凿就、背负九顶、面向三江,刻工线条流畅、比例匀称。佛座两壁尚有唐代石刻造像90余龛,堪称艺术佳品,极富研究价值,吸引着越来越多的中外游客参观游览。

Mount Emei, located at Emeishan City, Sichuan Province, is a natural scenic mountain with Buddhism playing its part. It occupies a special geographic location, and is known for its majestic nature sceneries typical topographic features, and well-preserved ecological environment. Even more remarkable are its being located at a transition zone where the world's biota integrates, and its housing 3,200 species of higher plants and 2,300 species of rare animals. These bestow on it certain characteristics particular to the reagion. The Golden Summit, 3,077 meters above sea level, offers four wonderful views: Sunrise, vast expanses of clouds, "Buddha's light", and the evening glow. At the center of Mount Emei, among dense woods and flowers, are the Elephant Bath Pond, Cave of Nine Old Men, and the Hongchunping Mountain Glen. In the past 2000 years, a rich heritage characterized by Buddhist culture has been created and accumulated here. Within the Beamless Hall of the Ten-Thousand-Year Temple, a hall with outstanding architectural features, towers a bronze statue of Samantabhadra. Cast in 980 in the Song Dynasty, it is 7.85 meters high, weighs 62 tons and is one of the important cultural relics of China. The Temple of Serving the Country is the site of important

佛事活动　Buddhist activities ↑

报国寺
Temple of Serving the Country ↓

峨眉灵猴
Monkeys in Mount Emei ↑

万年寺
Ten-Thousand-Year Temple →

Buddhist activities. The Tiger-Taming Temple, the largest temple in Mount Emei, is surrounded with ancient *nanmu*. Mount Emei is highly valuable in the study of history, aesthetics, in scientific researches and the popularization of science. It is also valuable as a tourist resort.

In the distance towers the Giant Buddha of Leshan, "the biggest buddha in the world". This scenic area is an organic combination of both cultural and natural heritages. Covering 2.5 square kilometers of land, it has the Tang Dynasty Giant Buddha in the center, with other scenic spots in the vicinity — Wuyou Mountain (Lidui) is hewn out by Li Bing, prefect of Sichuan in the Qin Dynasty; the groun of Han Dynasty rock-tombs, Buddhist statues of the Tang and Song; pagodas, temples and architectural structures of the Ming and Qing, etc. The world renowned 71-meter-high Giant Buddha is caryed on the rock face, with nine summits behind it and three rivers in front. The buddha is well proportioned and the carved lines flow smoothly. On both sides of its throne are 90 niches with statues carved in the Tang Dynasty. These exquisite pieces of art are valuable for researches and attract more and more Chinese and foreign tourists.

普贤铜像
A bronze statue of Samantabhadra ↑

凌云禅院
← Lingyun
Monastery

灵宝塔
Lingbao Pagoda

东坡楼
Tower of Su Dongpo →

睡佛倩影　The attractive Sleeping Buddha　↓

乐山大佛
Leshan Giant Buddha ↑

九曲栈道
The Nine-Twist plank trail →

116

汉代浮雕佛像
A Han Dynasty statue of a Buddha ↑

汉代陶房
Pottery house of Han ↑

麻浩崖墓（东汉）
A rock Tomb in Mahao（Eastern Han） ↓

中 国 其 他 风 景 名 胜
OTHER CHINESE SCENIC WONDERS

神 道
The Sacred Way ↑

碑 亭
Stale Pavilion ↓

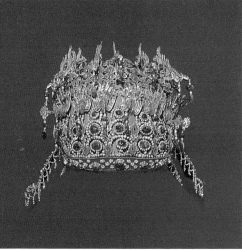

六龙六凤冠
Six-Dragon-Six-Phoenix Coronet ↑

明十三陵位于北京市昌平县境内
天寿山南麓,面积达 40 余平方公里,
因明代迁都北京后的十三个皇帝均葬
于此故称十三陵。自明永乐七年开始
建长陵,到清顺治初年建思陵,营建时
间前后达 200 余年。景区内主要包括
神道、各陵的地下建筑和地上建筑。
现正式开放的有长、定、昭三陵。十三
陵建筑风格典雅,气态庄严,是世界上
保存最完好、埋葬皇帝最多的帝王墓
葬群。

The Ming Tombs are located at the
southern foot of Tianshou Mountain in
Beijing's Changping County, occupying
an area of over 40 square kilometers. The
burial ground is so called because all
thirteen Ming emperors who ruled
China after the Chinese capital was
moved to Beijing were buried there.
Construction of the Ming Tombs took
over two centuries, starting from the
building of Changling in the 7th year of
the Ming Yong Le reign to the
completion of Siling in the early years of
the Qing Shun Zhi reign. The major
attractions of the Ming Tombs are Shen
Dao (the Sacred Way) and the ground
and underground architecture of the
tombs. Of the thirteen tombs, three are
currently open to the public, namely,
Changling, Dingling and Zhaoling. The
tombs exhibit an elegant yet dignified
architectural style. No other imperial
mausoleums in the world are so well
preserved and have entombed so many
imperial bodies as the Ming Tombs.

长陵鸟瞰
A bird's-eye view of Changling Mausoleum ↑

玄宫后殿
Back chamber of Underground Palace ↓

雍和宫位于北京市东城区。原为清代康熙第四子胤禛的雍亲王府。雍正帝继位后，原府改为佛教寺院。雍和宫规模宏大，巍峨壮观。共有七进院落，15座殿堂。各殿内有众多佛像、佛画、经书等，更以18米高檀木大佛像和金、银、铜、铁、锡制成的五百罗汉山和金丝楠木佛龛等"三绝"著称于世。

Yonghe Lamasery, located in the Dongcheng District of Beijing, was originally the residential palace of Prince Yong, the fourth son of Emperor Kang Xi of the Qing Dynasty. After Prince Yong succeeded to the throne and became Emperor Yong Zheng, the palace was converted into a Buddhist monastery. Yonghe Lamasery is a complex of grand scale and magnificent style. It consists of seven compounds with a total of

雍和宫所收藏金瓶
A golden jar in Yonghe Lamasery ↑

雍和宫全景
← A panorama view of Yonghe Lamasery

fifteen buildings, housing a large number of Buddhist statues, frescoes and scriptures. Its three famous treasures are the 18-meter-high statue of Buddha made of sandalwood, the Mountain of Five Hundred Arhats made of gold, silver, bronze, iron and tin, and the niche made of *nanmu*.

迈达拉佛
Statue of a Buddha →

大威德金刚像
Statue of a Vajra ↑

盘 山
Panshan Mountain

国家级风景名胜区盘山位于天津市蓟县(渔阳古城),为中国十五大名胜之一。以京东第一山而驰名。自三国时期到清末(公元3世纪到20世纪)为历代皇帝和名人的竞游之地。因寺院林立,佛教兴盛,自唐代便有"东五台山"之称。盘山主峰海拔864米,尤以五峰、八石和三盘为奇。遥望云海松涛,近观水石清奇,步步景色迷人,景景均有典故。清乾隆帝游历盘山后慨叹:早知有盘山,何必下江南!

Panshan Mountain, in Jixian County (historically known as Yuyang City) of Tianjin, is a National Scenic Area ranking among China's top fifteen scenic spots. It is also popularly known as the Number One Mountain of East Beijing and, from the Three-Kingdom Period through the late years of the Qing Dynasty (3rd to 20th centuries), had remained a favourite site of excursions by kings, emperors and celebrities. The mountain acquired the name of "Eastern Wutai Mountain" since the Tang Dynasty because of the multitude of Buddhist temples flourishing there. The summit of the mountain is 864 meters above sea level, and the five peake, eight rocks and three Pans (twined pine trees) are the mountain's most wonderful vistas. In a distance, one sees a full panorama of seas of clouds and clusters of waving pine trees, and close by, one marvels at crystal-clear waters and odd-shaped rocks. Every step leads to a picturesque scene, and every scene tells a legend. After a tour to Panshan Mountain, an enchanted Emperor Qian Long of the Qing Dynasty sighed: "If I had known there is a Panshan, I wouldn't have made tours to the South."

盘山秀色
A beautiful scenery of Mount Panshan ↓

天成寺
Tiancheng Monastery ↑

少林寺多宝佛塔
Pagoda of Pradhutaratna Buddha in
Shaolin Monastery →

大　钟　寺
The Big Bell Temple

　　大钟寺位于北京市海淀区。原名觉生寺,清雍正十一年(公元1733年)敕建。因于同年将华严钟(即永乐大钟,原在北京西郊万寿寺)移于此,遂名大钟寺。近年来又陆续收集中外珍贵古钟700余件,成立了古钟博物馆,占地面积22000平方米,建筑面积5500平方米,计有"战国编钟"、"古钟精品"、"古钟简史"、"永乐大钟"、"九亭钟园"、"外国古钟"等十个陈列单元。

　　The Big Bell Temple, located in Haidian District of Beijing, was built as Juesheng Temple (Temple of Awakening) in 1733 (11th year of the Qing Yong Zheng reign). It became popularly known as the Big Bell Temple that same year when the giant Huayan Bell (namely the Great Bell of Yong Le, originally housed in Wanshou Temple in the west suburb of Beijing) was moved there. The temple has been enriched in recent years by a collection of more than seven hundred invaluable ancient bells of Chinese and foreign origins. Having been turned into the Museum of Ancient Bells, it covers an area of 22,000 square meters with 5,500 square meters of floor space. The exhibition is devided into ten sections including "The Bell-Chime of the Warring States Period", "Distinguished Ancient Bells", "A Brief History of Ancient Bells", "The Yong Le Big Bell", "Foreign Ancient Bells" etc.

大钟寺古钟
← Ancient bell in Big Bell Temple

大钟寺门景
Gate of Big Bell Temple ↓

　　黄鹤楼位于湖北省武汉市,为中国三大名楼之一。始建于吴黄武二年(公元223年)。为历代文人骚客登临吟咏之胜地。留传至今的诗词过千,文赋逾百。其中以唐崔颢的"仙人已乘黄鹤去,此处空余黄鹤楼"诗句为最。黄鹤楼以楼体为主,因山就势,错落有致,形成了由楼、亭、轩、阁、坊、廊、榭等建筑群落和人文、自然景观融为一体的园林景观。

　　Huanghelou (Yellow Crane Tower) of Wuhan City, Hubei Province, is one of the three famous towers in China. Built in 223 the tower has been a spot most frequented by men of letters and, over the years, become the subject of more than a thousand poems and a hundred articles, the best known lines are "Long ago the immortal departed on the Yellow Crane, This Tower is all that's left." by Cui Hao of the Tang Dynasty. Merging perfectly with the natural scenery is the architectural complex of the tower — towers, pavilions, verandas, gateways and corridors etc. — built in proper distribution against the contours of the terrain.

黄鹤楼
Huanghelou（Yellow Crane Tower） ↓

黄鹤铜雕
Bronze yellow cranes ↑

牌 坊　Gateway　↑

　　石花洞又称十佛洞,位于北京市房山区。是中国华北
地区岩溶洞穴的代表。洞体共有七层(六、七层为地下暗
河),开放的一、二、三层洞道长 1900 米,洞底面积 18000 平
方米,计有 12 个高大厅堂、16 个洞室和 71 个形态各异的
支洞。洞内钟乳石多姿多彩,引人遐思。特别是大量月奶
石莲花为我国岩溶洞穴中首次发现。

　　Shihua Cave (Stone Flower Cave), also known as Cave of Ten
Buddhas, is in Fangshan District of Beijing. Typical of karst
caves found in north China, the cave has seven layers of cavity
(the sixth and seventh are underground rivers) and the first,
second and third layers, 1,900 meters in length and 18,000 square
meters in area, are open to tourists. The opened area has 12 high-
roofed caverns, 16 smaller caverns and 71 branch caverns of
different shapes. Stalactite formations in the cave are so
fascinatingly varied in form and shape that they never fail to
provoke imagination. Particularly worth nothing are the
encrinite formations, which are discovered for the first time in
Chine's karst caves.

火树银花
Fiery trees and silver flowers　→

蓬莱仙境
Fairyland of Penglai →

洞天三柱
← Three pillars in a cave

碧 海 山 庄
Beijing Green Sea Country Villa

北京碧海山庄位于北京市平谷县金海湖旅游区。距北京 85 公里。山庄背靠大金山，面对金海湖，附近有盘山、清东陵、京东大峡谷、湖洞水、独乐寺、轩辕黄帝陵、世外桃源、四座楼原始森林、丫吉山庙会多处风景区，是旅游、休闲的胜地。

Beijing Green Sea Country Villa is located in the Jinhai Lake Tourist Area of Pinggu County, about 85 kilometers from downtown Beijing. At the foot of Dajin Mountain and facing Jinhai Lake, the villa is close to numerous scenic spots, including Panshan Mountain, Eastern Qing Mausoleums, the Great Canyon of East Beijing, Hudongshui (Cave Lake), Dule Temple (Temple of Solitary Joy), Mausoleum of the Yellow Emperor, the Land of Peach Blossoms, Sizuolou Primeval Forest and Yajishan Temple Fair. It is a famous tourist attraction and holiday-makers' resort.

碧海山庄全景
A panorama view of Green Sea Country Villa ↓

雁栖湖黄昏
← Dusk at Yanqi Lake

　　雁栖湖位于北京怀柔县境内，因自古为春季大雁迁徙的栖息地而得名。景区内自然条件优越，植被覆盖率达80％，千年古槐与数百年的银杏至今生机盎然，枝叶繁茂。景区内人文景观遍布，东有金灯寺、普照寺；西有红螺寺、定慧寺。堪称为北京地区佛教界的重要丛林。

　　Yanqi Lake (Lake of Wild Geese's Sojourn), in Huairou County of Beijing, has derived its name for being a sojourn for the migrating wild geese in spring since time immemorial. The lake is located in an area of superior natural conditions, 80% covered by vegetation, where thousand-year-old Chinese scholartrees and centuries-old ginkgo trees are lush and flourishing. Sites of historical and cultural interest are found everywhere around the lake. To its east are Golden Lantern Temple and Universal Enlightenment Temple, to its west are Red Conch Temple and Temple of Samadhi and Mati. It may well be regarded a major Buddhist settlement in the Greater Beijing area.

雁栖湖一角
A corner of Yanqi Lake ↓

芙 蓉 洞
Hibiscus Cave

芙蓉洞位于重庆市武隆县江口镇。长江、乌江的水上交通及川黔、川鄂国道将其与重庆、涪陵等大中城市及长江三峡旅游区联系在一起。

芙蓉洞是一个大型洞穴,全长逾3公里,洞体高大,洞道蜿蜒。它是地下艺术宫殿和洞穴科学博物馆。洞内有巨大的石笋、石柱、石瀑和石幕,更有分布于洞壁及大小水池中的各种文石、方解石和石膏晶花。其中形成于水塘中的犬牙状和花朵状的方解石晶花、晶花上的浮筏石笋以及各种形状的石膏晶花在国内外洞穴中均是极其罕见的。

石膏晶花
Flower-shaped anthodite ↑

瑶池仙境
A mythical fairyland →

"巨幕"
← "Huge curtains"

芙蓉江漂流
Floating down the →
Hibiscus River

Located in Jiangkou Town, Wulong County of Chongqing City. Hibiscus Cave is connected to the cities of Chongqing and Fuling and the Three Gorges Tourist Area by the Yangtze and Wujiang rivers and the Sichuan-Guizhou and Sichuan-Hubei national roads.

The high and spacious cave twists along for 3 kilometers. It is a palace of underground art and a museum of speleology housing huge stalagmites, stalagnates and stone waterfalls and curtains. Aragonites, calsites, and anthodites decorate the cave walls and the numerous pools. The dog-teeth and flower-shaped calsites in the pools, the floating stalagmites on top of them and the flower-shaped gypsum formation are a rare sight in caves at home and abroad.

五 台 山
Wutai Mountain

佛光寺唐塑
Tang Dynasty sculptures in →
Temple of Buddhist Glory

五台山全景
A panorama view of Wutai Mountain ↓

龙泉寺汉白玉牌楼
Han Dynasty white marble archway in Dragon Spring Temple ↑

　　五台山位于山西省五台县。为中国四大佛教名山之
一。由五座山峰环抱而成。五峰高耸,峰顶平坦宽阔,故称
五台。五台山佛教历史悠久。相传在东汉永平十一年(公
元 68 年)开始修建寺庙,经各代兴修扩建,至今为止,尚保
存自唐代以来的各代寺庙 47 座。被誉为中国古建筑宝库。
五台山寺庙分为青、黄两种,既有汉传佛教,又有藏传佛教。
是研究中国古建筑、宗教、文化、艺术的宝地。五台山又名
清凉山,自然风光秀丽,气候凉爽宜人,是理想的避暑胜地。

　　Wutai Mountain, located at Wutai County, Shanxi Province,
consists of five platform-shaped peaks as its name indicates. One
of the four famous Buddhist shrines, the Wutai Mountain has a
long history of Buddhism. Temples began to be built on the
mountain in 68 (the 11th year of the Eastern Han Yong Ping
reign). With construction going on all through the dynasties the
mountain still boasts of 47 temples which were built since the
Tang Dynasty, forming a treasure-trove of ancient Chinese
architecture. These temples belong to the black and the yellow
sect — representing the Han and the Tibetan Buddhism. They
are a museum for the study of Chinese ancient architecture,
religion, culture and the arts. The mountain climate is cool and
pleasant, therefore Wutai Mountain is also called the Mountain
of Coolness. The pleasant weather and the natural scenery make
Wutai Mountain an ideal summer resort.

殊像寺文殊菩萨像
Statue of Manjusri in Shuxiang Temple →

桂 林
Guilin

桂林是中国著名的风景游览和历史文化名城。位于广西壮族自治区东北部,平均海拨 150 米,总面积 4195 平方公里。桂林地处亚热带,气候温和湿润,冬无严寒,夏无酷暑,风景宜人。

桂林的山,平地拔起,巍然兀立;桂林的水,曲折萦回,清澈如镜;桂林的洞,曲静幽深,石乳琳琅;桂林的石,千姿百态,形象万千。大自然塑造的奇峰、秀水、异洞、美石,深深地吸引着游人。自古以来,就有"桂林山水甲天下"的美誉。

The city of Guilin is reputed for its scenic beauty as well as being a city famed in history and culture. Located in the northeast of Guangxi Zhuang Autonomous Region it is 150 meters above sea level on an average with a total area of 4,195 square kilometers. This subtropical city, mild in temperature and moisture, never sees a scorching summer or a harsh winter but offers a picturesque scenery.

The mountains of Guilin, towering straight and high, appear to have popped up from the ground. The waters in Guilin, clear as a mirror, twist and turn in their course. Guilin has caves that are quiet and deep displaying a gallery of stalactite formations. And the rocks in Guilin have the most imaginative forms. Tourists marvel at the singular peaks, wonderful waters, spectacular caves and fantastic rocks of Guilin bestowed by Nature. Since ancient times, the city of Guilin is acclaimed for having the most beautiful scenery under Heaven.

桂林山水
Scenery of Guilin

武夷山位于福建省武夷山市南部,武夷山脉北段东南麓,面积70平方公里。素有"奇秀甲东南"之誉。

武夷山以丹山取胜,秀水称奇。典型的丹霞地貌,亿万年大自然的鬼斧神工,形成了秀拔奇伟,千姿百态,幽邃迷人的三十六峰,七十二洞,九十九岩和一百零八景点。澄碧清澈的九曲溪,山光水色融为一体,可谓"曲曲山回转,峰峰水抱流'。武夷山还是一座历史文化名山,南宋理学家朱熹曾驻足武夷山聚徒立说四十余载,成为东南文化学术中心。

Located to the south of Wuyishan City, Fujian Province, Mount Wuyi stands at the southeast of the northern stretch of the Wuyi mountain range. Covering an area of 70 square kilometers, Mount Wuyi is known as "the most attractive mountain in southeast China".

天游揽胜
Fascinating scenery on top of Mount Tianyou ↓

玉女峰
Jade Maiden Peak ↑

The cliffs and waters of Mount Wuyi are exceptionally outstnding. The workings of Nature of a typical Danxia landform have left behind 36 peaks, 72 caves, 99 distinguished rocks and 108 scenic sites — all splendid sights with varying shapes and postures, uncomparable grandeur or charming elegance. The Stream with Nine Turnings are emerald green and crystal clear. The complementary beauty of mountain and stream is aptly described by the lines: "Every turning is flanked by slope. Every peak is encircled with water." Mount Wuyi is known for its cultural activities in history too. Zhu Xi, a philosopher of Southern Song who taught disciples for 40 years in Mount Wuyi, made it an academic center of southeast China.

　　"世界之窗"位于深圳湾旅游度假区西部,毗邻"锦绣中华"和"中国民俗文化村"。以仿美旧金山的"金门大桥"为起点,首先进入亚洲区,东方四大奇迹之一的柬埔寨吴哥窟、印尼的婆罗浮屠,印度的泰姬陵,日本的桂离宫尽收眼底。穿过风情浓郁的东南亚水乡,又进入大洋洲区的悉尼歌剧院、毛利民居等。在景区中轴线上分布着埃菲尔铁塔、凯旋门、四大洲喷泉、圣.米歇尔修道院。地毯式的园林两侧汇集了欧洲各地、各时代充满人文气质的景致和建筑。非洲区展现沙漠风情、古老文化和原始部落的生活。美洲区以壮丽的大自然景观大峡谷、大瀑布为起点,使人历览以总统山、纽约曼哈顿为代表的现代文明,最后回归到复活节岛那斯卡图线等神秘氛围中。

　　"世界之窗"的景观精美绝伦,其世界民俗风情表演更

是引人入胜。每当夜幕降临,世界广场一片欢腾,近200米长的浮雕墙上烟花瀑布喷珠溅玉,艺术狂欢大游行令人热血沸腾。"世界与您共欢乐"的主题表现得淋漓尽致。

　　"您给我一天,我将给您一个美妙的世界"。

Window of the World is located in the west of Shenzhen Bay Holiday Resort and adjacent to Splendid Land of China and Village of Chinese Folk Customs. An imitation Golden Gate Bridge of San Franscisco, USA at the entrance leads to the Asian District where one sees Angkor Wat of Cambodia — one of the four wonders of the East, Borobudur of Indonesia, Taj Mahal of India and Katsura Rikyu of Japan. Passing among rivers and lakes of Southeast Asia, one comes to the Sydney Opera House and the abodes of the Maori people of Oceania. On the axis of the Resort are the Eiffel Tower, the Arch of Truimph, fountains of the four continents and St. Michel's Convent. European

architect
with law
stretch o
America
Waterfa
Mount F
returns t

The i
World a
showing
200-mete
highligh
displayin
rejoices
"Give

...sceneries line both sides of a garden carpeted ...owers. The African District is represented by a ... ancient culture and primeval tribe life. The ...ct starts with the Grand Canyon and the ...lowed by modern civilization represented by ...e and Manhanttan in New York and finally ...ystery of Easter Island, and Nazca Lines.

...ly constructed scenic spots in Window of the ...ating. Even more so are the performances ...oms of peoples in the world. At nightfall, the ...Wall of Relief Sculptures lit up by fireworks ...ubilation of the jolly parade on the square, ...full the main theme of the Resort — "the world ...".

...ay, and I'll give you a world of wonders."

世界之窗广场
The square in front of Window of the World ↑

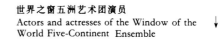

世界之窗狂欢之夜
← A carnival of Window of the World

世界之窗五洲艺术团演员
Actors and actresses of the Window of the ↓
World Five-Continent Ensemble

天下奇秀雁荡山
The Wondrous Yandang Mountain

雁荡山位于浙江省温州市北部，方圆450平方公里，拥有550多个景点，素有"海上名山"、"寰中绝胜"之誉。它以奇峰怪石、古洞石室、飞瀑流泉、层峦叠嶂称胜。因主峰雁湖岗上有着结满芦苇的湖荡，年年南飞的秋雁栖宿于此，因而得名"雁荡山"。

沈括在《梦溪笔谈》中载："峭拔怪险，上耸千尺，穹崖巨谷，不类他山。"堪称"天下奇秀"。

Located to the north of Wenzhou, Zhejiang Province and covering an area of 450 square kilometers, Yandang Mountain encompasses over 550 scenic sights. Known as the "famous mountain on the sea" and "the unique spot under Heaven" it is noted for its sheer peaks, grotesque rocks, ancient caves, cascading waterfalls, flowing springs and verdant trees. Its main peak is a place with reed marshes where flocks of south-bound swan geese stop in autumn. Hence the name Yandang (swan goose and marsh).

In his *Dream Stream Essays* Shen Kuo (1031-1095) records: "Cliffs sheer and bizarre soaring straight up and towering rocks and unfathomable valleys make it quite a unique mountain." It truely lives up to its fame as "a wondrous mountain under Heaven".

雁荡山大龙湫
Big Dragon Waterfall in Yandang Mountain ↑

接客僧
"Guest-Receiving Monk" ↓

音乐喷泉
← Music-controlled spring

北海银滩与周围的涠洲岛度假区、星岛湖度假区、冠头岭国家森林公园、英罗湾红树林国家保护区、白龙珍珠城以及古文物、古建筑观光区、近代观光区组成资源丰富的北海旅游区。

Located at Beihai City, Guangxi Zhuag Automous Region, the Beihai Yintan National Holiday Resort is characterized by having a long flat beach, fine white sand, pleasant warm water, soft waves, and for being shark free. The resort offers night-time swimming, surfing, aquatic sports, beech golf, volley and basketball games as well as night-time music fountains. It is an ideal spot for tourists and holiday-makers.

Beihai Tourist Area consists of Beihai Yintan National Holiday Resort, Weizhou Island Holiday Resort, Xingdao Lake Resort, Guantou Ridge National Forest Park, Yinluo Bay National Preservation of Mangrove Forest, Bailong Pearl City, the ancient cultural relics and architecture area and the modern tourist sites area etc.

北海银滩国家旅游度假区位于广西壮族自治区北海市。具有"滩平长，沙细白、水温清、浪柔软、无鲨鱼"的特点。银滩夜泳、冲浪、水上运动及沙滩高尔夫球、沙滩排球和篮球、夜间音乐喷泉等项目为世人所熟知和爱好，是度假疗养佳境，观光旅游圣地。

北海银滩公园一角
A corner of Beihai Yintan Park ↓

星湖风景名胜区
Xinghu Scenic Area

星湖风景名胜区位于广东省肇庆市,是第一批国家重点风景名胜区,已有一千多年的旅游开发历史。由集杭州西湖之水、桂林阳朔之山美景于一体的七星岩景区和有"北回归线上的绿宝石"之称的鼎湖山景区组成。以山清、水秀、岩奇、洞幽而著称。地处北回归

星湖七星岩"水月岩云"
"A moon in the pool and clouds around the peak" — a scene at Seven-Star Crags in Xinghu Scenic Area ↓

线沙漠带上及城市近郊的鼎湖山，却能保有蕴含 1700 多种高等植物而十分珍贵的自然林（原始森林），成为第一个国家级自然保护区，1978 年被联合国教科文组织认定为世界自然保护区和"人与生物圈"定位科研地。

Located in Zhaoqing City, Guangdong Province and with a whole thousand years' history in tourism, Xinghu Scenic Area is among the first batch of national key scenic areas. It consists of two parts. One being the Seven-Star Crags Scenic Area which is an integration of the charm of the West Lake in Hangzhou and the beauty of the mountains in Yangshuo, Guilin. The other is the Dinghu Mountain Scenic Area known as an emerald on the Tropic of Cancer. The attraction of Xinghu Scenic Area is its magnificent mountains, lovely waters, outstanding rocks and secluded caves. Although located in the desert zone of the Tropic of Cancer and in the near suburb of a city, Dinghu Mountain Scenic Area houses 1,700 species of higher plants and very precious primeval forests, making it China's first state-level nature reserve. In 1978 it was approved by UNESCO as a world nature reserve and a fixed location for scientific researches of "man and biosphere".

鼎湖山的龙潭飞瀑
A waterfall cascades into the dragon pool →
— waterfall in Dinghu Mountain

鼎湖山
Dinghu Mountain ↓

金石滩国家旅游度假区
Jinshitan Holiday Resort

金石滩旅游度假区位于辽宁省大连市东北端黄海之滨。度假区三面环海,由两个半岛及半岛间的开阔腹地和海水浴场组成。长达8公里的东部海岸线,山海相间,震旦纪、寒武纪地貌和古生物化石形成了近百处景观,被国际地质界称为"海上石林",其中龟裂石形成于6亿年前,是目前世界发现的最大的奇石。

金石滩度假区旅游设施完善。金石锚地国际俱乐部,蓝梦庄园,玫瑰庄园等提供了良好旅游条件。金石滩高尔夫球场第一期18球洞已正式开放。海上娱尔项目包括帆板、摩托艇、快艇、游艇、海上滑翔伞、垂钓等多项活动。国际狩猎场提供了狩猎、飞碟、小口径等竞技活动。形成了旅游设施齐全,旅游产品特色突出,具有浓郁田园风光的旅游景区。

Jinshitan Holiday Resort is located on the coast of the Yellow Sea at the northeast of Dalian City, Liaoning Province. Surrounded on three sides by the sea, the area encompasses two peninsulas, the region in between and a sea-bathing area. The 8-kilometer-long mountainous east coast, belonging to the Sinian and Cambrian landform, houses close to a hundred paleofossil tourist attractions which are acclaimed by the international geological circles as a "stone forest on the sea". The Polygonal Rock, formed 6 hundred million years ago, is the largest of its kind discovered in the world.

国际游艇俱乐部
International Yachting Club ↑

Jinshitan Holiday Resort has many tourist facilities including Jinshi Maodi International Club, Blue Dream Villa and Rose Villa. The golf course has 18 holes opened to the public in its first stage. Other entertainments on the sea include windsurfing, moterboat, speedboat, paraglider and fishing. The International Hunting Ground offers hunting, Frisbee, small-bore shooting, etc. The Jinshitan Holiday Resort is a tourist spot with a rich pastoral flavor and a complete range of facilities. It also has many outstanding products for the tourists to enjoy and purchase.

金石友谊高尔夫俱乐部
Jinshi Friendship Golf Club ↓

京工商广临字 97035 号

责任编辑：沈根发　　**Editor:** Shen Genfa
装帧设计：孙　杰　　**Design and layout:** Sun Jie
英文翻译：喻璠琴　　**Translator:** Yu Fanqin
校　　对：陈　棣　　**Proof Reading:** Chen Di

图书在版编目（CIP）数据

世界遗产在中国/游琪主编
－北京：旅游教育出版社，1997.5
ISBN 7－5637－0702－6

Ⅰ.世… Ⅱ.游… Ⅲ.名胜古迹－中国－摄影集
Ⅳ.K92 8.7－64

中国版本图书馆 CIP 数据核字(97) 第 04951 号

世界遗产在中国

游　琪　主编

旅游教育出版社
（北京市朝阳区定福庄南里 1 号）
外文印刷厂制版印刷
新华书店经销
＊　　＊　　＊
开本 889×1194 毫米 1/16　9.25 印张　17 千字　正文彩图 198 幅
1997 年 5 月第 1 版　1997 年 5 月第 1 次印刷
印数：1—7000 册　　定价：118.00 元